D1685897

B.S.U.C. - LIBRARY

00211382

Italo Calvino:
Eros and Language

Italo Calvino: Eros and Language

Tommasina Gabriele

Rutherford • Madison • Teaneck
Fairleigh Dickinson University Press
London and Toronto: Associated University Presses

© 1994 by Associated University Presses, Inc.

All rights reserved. Authorization to photocopy items for internal or personal use, or the internal or personal use of specific clients, is granted by the copyright owner, provided that a base fee of $10.00, plus eight cents per page, per copy is paid directly to the Copyright Clearance Center, 27 Congress Street, Salem, Massachusetts 01970. [0-8386-3531-8/94 $10.00 + 8¢ pp, pc.]

Associated University Presses
440 Forsgate Drive
Cranbury, NJ 08512

Associated University Presses
25 Sicilian Avenue
London WC1A 2QH, England

Associated University Presses
P.O. Box 338, Port Credit
Mississauga, Ontario
Canada L5G 4L8

The paper used in this publication meets the requirements of the American National Standard for Permanence of Paper for Printed Library Materials Z39.48-1984.

Library of Congress Cataloging-in-Publication Data

Gabriele, Tommasina, 1962–
    Italo Calvino : eros and language / Tommasina Gabriele.
    p. cm
    English and Italian.
    Includes bibliographical references and index.
    ISBN 0-8386-3531-8
    1. Calvino, Italo—Criticism and interpretation. I. Title.
PQ 4809.A45Z722 1994
853′.914—dc20
                                            92-55106
                                          CIP

BATH SPA UNIVERSITY
COLLEGE
NEWTON PARK LIBRARY

Class No.
853·914 CAL G

DISCARD

Phil Dutch

PRINTED IN THE UNITED STATES OF AMERICA

per nonna Loreta

amore ed erotismo
non possono essere scritti
con le parole
dell'amore e dell'erotismo

love and eroticism
cannot be written about
with the words
of love and eroticism

—from a letter by Calvino
to Bianca Garufi,
now in *I libri degli altri*

Contents

Acknowledgments

My thanks go first and foremost to Franco Ferrucci, who made this study possible by alerting me to the shortage of criticism on eros in Calvino's work. I am very grateful for his sensitive reading and unstinting support. I would also like to extend my thanks to my friend and colleague, Luisa Gozzi, for her advice on translation, as well as to Anthony Gabriele, for his invaluable computer knowledge. I am also very grateful to Wheaton College in Massachusetts for its contribution toward my research costs. Finally, my deepest thanks to Sara Weiss and to my husband, Kenneth W. Smith, who have generously and uncomplainingly sustained me, day in and day out, in this and in all things.

Except where indicated, all translations are my own.

Quotations from *Gli amori difficili* (Turin: Einaudi, 1970), *Cosmicomiche vecchie e nuove* (Milan: Garzanti, 1984), *Sotto il sole giaguaro* (Milan: Garzanti, 1986), *Una pietra sopra* (Turin: Einaudi, 1980) and Calvino's untitled essay in the special edition, "Otto domande sull'erotismo," in *Nuovi argomenti* 51–52 (July–Oct. 1961) are translated and reprinted by permission of Wylie, Aitken and Stone, Inc. Selections from my article, "Literature as Education and the Near-Perfect Protagonist: Narrative Structure in *Il barone rampante*," are reprinted by permission of *Stanford Italian Review.*

Italo Calvino:
Eros and Language

1

Toward an Understanding of Calvino

Italo Calvino figures on the international literary scene as a complex and oftentimes controversial author. A quick glance at a bibliographical printout of the 1980s reveals that more than twice the amount of critical studies on Calvino emerged in that decade than in the three preceding decades. Nor can this avalanche of scholarly interpretations be explained away by the mythicizing effect of Calvino's demise in 1985, for the level of critical interest had been growing steadily in the decade before his death. Calvino is considered by many to be one of the greatest writers of our time, and while slashing criticisms of his works still do on occasion surface (the harshest one that comes to mind, written by James Gardner, appeared immediately following his death), they are growing increasingly rare.[1] To this effect, A. H. Carter writes,

> When Italo Calvino died of a stroke in September of 1985 at the age of 61, Italy mourned the loss of her most prominent and respected living author. Ordinary readers knew his *Italian Folktales*, scholars had studied his works, and more than one critic has suggested that Calvino would be receiving the Nobel prize one year or another. The death was sudden, unforeseen, surprising—qualities that often characterize Calvino's fiction.[2]

Greatly influenced by his activities as intellectual, critic, translator, essayist, and as editor, since 1947, for the Torino-based publishing house Einaudi, Calvino's writing spans more than four decades and is characterized—as Carter suggested—by innovation and a spirit of constant thematic, narrative and linguistic renewal, as well as a sensitivity to the intellectual and literary milieu around him. Far from constantly regenerating one theme, or one style for that matter, Calvino has intrigued and perplexed readers and critics alike by producing unexpected and provocative texts and keeping abreast of modern literary and critical—

and even technological—trends.[3] Critics and scholars consistently and repeatedly highlight Calvino's creative diversity and literary experimentation, and these remain perhaps the only two descriptions of Calvino's works upon which the critical world almost unanimously concurs. Perhaps Calvino himself has best expressed these qualities in this excerpt from his (recognizably?) tongue-in-cheek address to the Reader who is reading Calvino's *Se una notte d'inverno un viaggiatore*:

> Ti prepari a riconoscere l'inconfondibile accento dell'autore. No. Non lo riconosci affatto. Ma, a pensarci bene, chi ha mai detto che questo autore ha un accento inconfondibile? Anzi, si sa che è un autore che cambia molto da libro a libro. E proprio in questi cambiamenti si riconosce che è lui.[4]

> You get ready to recognize the author's unmistakable accent. No. You don't recognize it at all. But, if you really think about it, who ever said that this author has an unmistakable accent? Rather, it's common knowledge that he is an author who changes a great deal from book to book. And it is precisely in these changes that he is recognizable.

As is often the case with significant writers, attempts to define and understand Calvino's work and theory of literature abound; however, they are constantly thwarted by Calvino's chameleonic and provocative style. Attempts at a serious definition and understanding of Calvino are further foiled by his large output of self-commentary in the form of interviews, essays, and introductions to his texts (e.g., to the 1960 trilogy, *I nostri antenati*, perhaps the most famous, and to a middle school edition of *Il barone rampante* in 1965, to mention a few).[5] In fact, rather than clarifying Calvino's opinions and theories, this output further confuses the issue because Calvino has on occasion, be it at the time of publication or years afterwards, contradicted himself or at very least detached himself from some of his self-commentary. Here are some examples of such undermining gestures:

1) Interviews. Thomson asserts that

> Calvino has always, in fact, been hostile to definite interpretations. Elsewhere he has said: "I agree to my books being read as existential or as structural works, as Marxist or neo-Kantian, Freudianly or Jungianly: but above all I am glad when I see that no single key will turn the lock."[6]

2) Introductions. A. H. Carter writes,

In my interview with Calvino in Paris, 21 November 1969, he spoke of the need for openness in critical readings; in a letter, 24 January 1970, he affirmed that he had abolished the preface [which appeared in the 1960 edition of *I nostri antenati*] because he had tired of it.[7]

He also never republished the notes and introduction to the 1965 *Barone rampante*.

3) Essays. In 1960 Calvino wrote,

> Forse potrei far finta che la mia personale idea della letteratura sia una scuola ... ma come fare a definirla se finora la mia preoccupazione è stata sempre quella di smentire le definizioni che i critici hanno dato di me?[8]

> Maybe I could make believe that my own personal idea of literature is a school ... but how would I define it, if my primary concern till now has been to disprove the definitions the critics have given of me?

In 1980, in his preface to *Una pietra sopra*, Calvino observed,

> La ricorrente inclinazione a formulare dei programmi generali, testimoniati da questi scritti, è stata sempre controbilanciata dalla tendenza a dimenticarmene subito e a non tornarci più sopra. Ci si può chiedere per chi mai li formulassi, questi piani d'operazioni: non per me, dato che nel mio lavoro personale di scrittore quasi mai mettevo in pratica ciò che avevo predicato.[9]

> My recurring tendency to formulate general plans, as these writings testify, has always been counterbalanced by my tendency to quickly forget about them and not bother with them again. One might ask oneself who on earth I formulated these plans of operation for? Not for myself, given that in my personal work as a writer I hardly ever practiced what I preached.

The title of the collection of essays from which I have just quoted is also significant. It translates approximately as "having exhausted a certain issue," as "closing the book on it"—as if publishing an edition of these collected essays were a way for Calvino to have done with them, to mark as definitively closed certain stages of his past.[10]

Such determined elusiveness has created a mine field for critics and has rendered the attempt to individuate a "constant"— a difficult endeavor in any case—and to characterize Calvino's work a very tricky proposition indeed. As tricky as it is tempting. Not surprisingly, differences in opinion flourish. For example,

Barilli in 1959 claimed that in Calvino, "la relazione con le cose è lineare, 'fotografica,' priva di implicazioni ontologiche, né si propone di introdurre a un nuovo ordine fenomenico" (The relation with things is linear, "photographic," completely without ontological implications, nor is the introduction of a new phenomenal order proposed).[11] Richard Andrews, in 1984, stated in direct contradiction to Barilli:

> The one constant of Calvino's fiction, which in most respects has been exhiliratingly variable and inconstant, is that he has never been trapped (as he would see it) into a mere photographic representation of the world in which he lives.[12]

Another noteworthy difference of opinion is Ricci's assertion, "The theme of affirmation via negation is discussed by Calvino in 'Il midollo del leone,' and negativity, I should like to suggest, forms the basis for all the author's work"[13] as contrasted to Francesco Guardiani's article, "Optimism Without Illusions," in which optimism in Calvino is considered a "spring for action," a "desire to know."[14] Guardiani affirms, "The rampant baron is the most powerful symbol of Calvino's optimism without illusions."[15]

Without lingering excessively on such controversies, for they are so prolific as to constitute a study apart, I feel it would be nonetheless beneficial to an understanding of Calvino to mention briefly some of the ongoing pivotal polemics which have engaged dozens of critics over the years. One of the most significant controversies that continues to divide scholars dates back to Vittorini's description of Calvino's work as "realismo a carica fiabesca" and "fiaba a carica realistica" (realism infused with fairytale and fairytale infused with realism).[16] De Lauretis observes,

> It is often said that Calvino's writings oscillate between two extremes, one being sociopolitical involvement resulting in a style that may be called "neorealist," and the other the fantastic or escapist literature of works like *Le cosmicomiche* or the recent *Le città invisibili* (1972). This polarity is believed to be caused by divided impulses or irreconcilable interests in the author.[17]

In fact, some identify in Calvino a neorealist rather than a fantastic strain, while others see him as a "realist." Some see elements of fantasy in all of Calvino's *opus* and consider him to be fundamentally a writer of fantasy; still others find that a combination of realism and fantasy pervades all his fiction.[18] This fantasy vs. realism polemic will be explored further on, especially in its relation to another long-raging controversy: Calvino—escapist or *engagé*?

Also much disputed is Calvino's relation to, and use of, post-modernist literary theory and metaliterary, metanarrative techniques, which have been traced as far back as his *I nostri antenati* by Cannon and others. Cannon feels that Calvino's use of these techniques indicates that he participates in, and suffers from, modern literature's uncertainty of its ability to generate meaning, to be meaningful, while others believe Calvino can represent modern literature's crisis without being swallowed up by it.[19] To say it with R. Andrews:

> Words and signs, it is true, have no intrinsic meaning, but nor does the world as a whole—until it is selectively interpreted into words and signs. Statements of this sort become more explicit in later books like *Cosmicomiche* and *Le città invisibili* but they are implicit here [in *Il cavaliere inesistente*] too. The impossibility of writing is successfully written about.[20]

In essence, many aspects of Calvino's use of postmodernist technique and theory are issues of contention, even the seriousness and prevalence of that usage. Gardner, in a scathing judgment, declares Calvino susceptible to following fashionable Derrida-influenced and deconstructionist criticism.[21] Palmieri insists, on the other hand, that

> gli strumenti critici (semiotica, linguistica, filosofia del linguaggio, teoria della critica ecc.) nella narrativa di Calvino non giocano un ruolo tanto massiccio e programmatico come certi critici si ostinano a sostenere, ma piuttosto suggestivo nell'accezione più ampia del termine; il rapporto con la semiotica è molto più sfumato di quanto non si dica.[22]

> critical methodologies (semiotics, linguistics, the philosophy of language, critical theory, etc.) do not play as substantial and programmatic a role in Calvino's narrative as some critics persist in maintaining, but rather an evocative role, in the broadest sense of the term; the relationship with semiotics is much less direct than is claimed.

Calvino himself states, in an interview with Thomson, "[I don't] subscribe wholeheartedly to all the theoretical ideas as they appear in my books, and I admit that there is even a sort of satire on interpretations in my writing, especially in *If on a winter's night a traveler.*"[23]

Must we conclude, then, that creative diversity and literary experimentation are Calvino's only "unifying" traits, or at least the only ones the critical world can as much as is possible agree upon?[24] Perhaps not. In the avalanche of dispute, commentary and exegesis, there surface some recurring themes, some *key words*, one might say, some increasingly familiar observations that form, if not unanimous concurrence, at least resounding echoes worth investigating.

The first discernible echo is the prevalence in Calvino's work of *contrasting* elements. Considered as a very broad category, "contrast" as a literary device includes such synonyms and related ideas as opposition, antithesis, counterpoint and symmetry (in its definition as opposition of two elements or as geometry) and permeates Calvino's work at all levels: linguistic, thematic, narrative, structural and "actantial."[25] Many fine studies have been devoted entirely to some aspect or angle of this broad category, while numerous others mention the element of contrast tangentially. Almansi's study, "Il mondo binario di Italo Calvino," finds the recurring geometrical structures in Calvino's texts to be negatively limiting, redeemed only by what Almansi calls the "Gnac factor"—"anti-ordine, anti-binario, anti-simmetrico" (antiorder, antibinary, antisymmetric).[26] Taking a positive view of Calvino's oppositional structures, I. T. Olken, whose book *With Pleated Eye and Garnet Wing* is subtitled *Symmetries of Italo Calvino*, emphasizes the harmonizing effects of patterns. Olken observes, "Contrasts and antitheses are a constant in Calvino's themata."[27] De Lauretis isolates an "essentially binary opposition, at both the thematic and actantial levels" in some of Calvino's works.[28] In essence, Calvino seems to have structured and conceived *all* of his fiction around a structure of contrasting elements. The most obvious paradigm of "contrast" and opposition is, as many have pointed out, the figure of Medardo, "il visconte dimezzato," who is divided into a cruel half and a righteous half by a cannon ball during a Turkish war. As is Calvino's wont, the novel exploits the implications of the image he has created to their humorous and philosophical extreme: the evil half destroys things by halving them and flies off into meditations on the merits of being half, while the "good" Medardo, as Olken puts it, "literally kill[s] . . . with kindness."[29]

A few of the countless possible illustrations are these in the trilogy *I nostri antenati*, which is very blatantly organized around an oppositional symmetrical structure. In *Il cavaliere inesistente*, for example, Agilulfo does not exist, while Gurdulù tries to transform himself into anything that does exist, even soup or a cadaver. In *Il barone rampante*, being above the ground symbolizes freedom, while being on the ground means captivity, submission to societal convention; and this is true for the young fruit-thieves who play in the trees, for young Violante on her horse, as well as for Cosimo.[30]

As regards linguistic contrast, particularly evident in *Le cosmicomiche*, various illustrations are provided by F. Bernardini Napoletano and De Lauretis. The latter critic observes:

> Both lexicon and syntax are subject to a deformation consisting mainly in the juxtaposition of the common "spoken language" usage and a highly specialized, scientific or literary language. The specific terminology of art criticism, for example, is followed in the same sentence by the imprecise idiomatic catchall words of daily speech: . . . "il mio ritratto tradotto in un sistema ritmico di volumi e striscie e colori *e roba dura*."[31]

Bernardini Napoletano explores linguistic opposition in depth in her chapter, "Letteratura e scienza, linguaggio poetico e linguaggio scientifico ne *Le cosmicomiche* e *Ti con zero*" in *I segni nuovi di Italo Calvino*.[32] I defer to these linguistic analyses and to the reader's own curiosity to uncover other instances of "contrast," too numerous to exhaust within the scope of the present study.

Opposition, symmetry, antithesis, counterpoint: all these subcategories of the general device we call "contrast" offer to author and reader alike manifold creative and interpretive possibilities, a rich territory for the pursuit of meanings, associations, and interweaving motifs. Images of "contrast" have also been exploited by Calvino for their humorous, ironic potential, for their *game* potential. In fact, a second resounding "echo," another "unifying trait" is the predominance of games. Everywhere one searches, one finds games, from Pin's pistol game and Libereso's provocative gifts to a scandalized Maria-nunziata ("Un giorno, Adamo"), to the soldier's tentative game of seduction ("l'avventura di un soldato"), to Qfwfq's gambling and bets with Il Decano (k)yK, his brawl *à la* Old West with Tenente Fenimore and the particularly relevant "Giochi senza fine," to Marco Polo and Kubla Khan's game of chess, to Calvino's own wicked game with the Reader and readers in *Se una notte*. Everywhere in his texts are games of all sorts and all tones: narrative games, visual games, numerical games (*Le città invisibili*), metaliterary and linguistic games. Even deadly games, such as in the *incipits* of *Se una notte* and in *Il castello*. Games permeate all of Calvino's fiction. Their prevalence is remarkable and their importance indisputable.

While play has many functions, in relation to "contrast" it furnishes the energy which sets the elements in binary opposition in motion. Games create the tension, the friction; they provide ideological, thematic and especially plot movement in Calvino's fiction, for games have by definition built-in components of competitiveness and suspense, of victory and defeat, and of stretching a participant's abilities in a specified area. "Giochi senza fine" and "Quanto scommettiamo?" perhaps best exemplify this, for the betting game and the hydrogen marble game trigger the narrative movement, sustain its speed, and provide encounters that highlight the differences and similarities of the opponents.

Although I believe an exhaustive discussion of play has not yet been fully undertaken, articles on various aspects of it exist. For example, G. Scalise talks about a doubting Palomar in his "The Game of Palomar."[33] G. Dossena in "Sillabari, lipogrammi e rime per l'occhio" explores Calvino's fascination with word games and his association, to this end, with OULIPO (Ouvroir de Littérature Potentielle). Dossena says, "che Calvino amasse certi giochi di parole è stato testimoniato da Massimo Piattelli Palmarini ('Corriere della Sera' 29-9-85)"; and, "per tornare alla Francia, lì alcuni sanno che Calvino giocava con Queneau e con Perec e gli altri nelle sedute dell'Oulipo" (that Calvino loved certain word games has been testified by Massimo Piattelli Palmarini ("Corriere della Sera" 29-9-85); [and,] to return to France, there some know that Calvino played with Queneau and Perec and others at Oulipo sessions).[34] Warren F. Motte, Jr. has further researched Calvino's association with the OULIPO (which he joined in 1973), with *ars combinatoria* and with play. I refer to his articles, "Calvino's Combinatorics" and "Telling Games."[35] Other fine studies have appeared on Calvino's treatment of literature as an *ars combinatoria*, and especially in reference to *Il castello*.[36]

On several occasions Calvino himself has brought up the idea of play and in at least two instances he has addressed the issue in reference to one of his most beloved authors, Ariosto. Olken quotes Calvino's affirmation that he himself approached "the novel of action and political engagement"

> with the same attitude . . . with which Ariosto approached the romances of chivalry. Ariosto sees these romances through a veil of irony and fantastic transfiguration, but nonetheless, he never undervalues the fundamental virtues they express, never debases the idea of man that animates them, even if there remains nothing for him to do but change them into a brilliant, fluid game.[37]

Olken comments:

> The brilliant fluid game is not a sign of detachment on the part of the writer ["Is my love of Ariosto escapism? No."]; on the contrary, it is a highly personal expression of the need to dramatize human error and achievement, one of the ways in which the uses of the past can be taught and learned and understood.[38]

In a radio broadcast on the occasion of the five hundredth anniversary of Ariosto's birth, in 1974, Calvino says,

> The word "game" has come up several times in this talk, but we must not forget that games, whether of children or grown-ups, always have a serious basis. First and foremost they are techniques for training the faculties and attitudes that will be required for life.[39]

The pivotal role games play in Calvino's texts is perhaps associated with another of those "echoes" mentioned earlier. Various observations made by critics identify Calvino's creations as literature of demystification. That is, Calvino, in a tongue-in-cheek tone, using an ironic slant, succeeds in undercutting the seriousness of those social and literary conventions which he also succeeds in accurately portraying. This demystifying effect goes hand-in-hand perhaps with Calvino's attempts to create new myths, more authentic ways of living or viewing reality. By undermining or deriding present "systems," Calvino seems to be clearing the ground to make room for new and fresh insights into humanity's current condition. However, his "mythicizing" is perhaps not so apparent or easy to prove as his "demystifying," and seems to have received less attention from scholars. Here are several clear illustrations of his achievements in the realm of demystification. In *Marcovaldo*, for example, alongside the depiction of urban corruption and pollution, Calvino also, through the lovable but haplessly inept protagonist, undermines the Romantic notion of a "return to nature"; Marcovaldo knows nothing about the natural world, as is evidenced by his mishaps with the mushrooms and pigeons. Marcovaldo has not been transplanted from a rural environment into an urban one; rather, he chases a rather indefinite dream of paradise. The introduction to the 1966 edition, most probably written by Calvino, corroborates this point and summarizes as well some of the demystifying intentions of the Marcovaldo short stories:

L'idillio "industriale" è preso di mira allo stesso tempo dell'idillio "campestre": non solo non è possibile un "ritorno indietro" nella storia, ma anche quell' "indietro" non è mai esistito, è un'illusione. L'amore per la natura di Marcovaldo è quello che può nascere solo in un uomo di città: per questo non possiamo sapere nulla d'una sua provenienza extracittadina; questo estraneo alla città è il cittadino per eccellenza.[40]

The "industrial" idyll is targeted at the same time as the "country" idyll; not only is "turning back" in history not possible, but even that "back" never existed and is an illusion. Marcovaldo's love of nature is the kind that can only spring up in a city man: for this reason, we can know nothing of any of his possible origins outside the city; this stranger to the city is the city dweller *par excellence*.

As other evidence of this prevalent technique of demystification, Maria Corti gives the image of the upside-down Orlando in *Il Castello*, for whom a return to reason has a totally different meaning from what it had in the classical tale: "il compito della ragione diventa la lettura demistificante dell'universo, e la vertigine della testa in giù nell'affabile carta del Biondo Penduto ne è bellissima immagine iconica" (The demystifiying reading of the universe becomes reason's task, and the vertigo of the head down in the affable card of the Hanged Blonde Man is a beautiful iconic image of it).[41]

Another text which has spurred many observations of demystification is *Le cosmicomiche*. Several critics have noticed, for example, that the theories that preface most of the stories differ from each other and are contradictory. A. H. Carter underlines the hypothetical nature of science, so often considered in these technologically advanced times as the ultimate authority on material truth: "By exploring the hypothetical nature of both fantasy and science, *Cosmicomics* suggests that they have more in common than we may have realized."[42] In this way, Calvino demystifies science, as well as the scientific "bases" of his stories. L. Guj quotes De Lauretis—

> Per il fatto stesso di metterla [la scienza] sullo stesso piano della fiaba, del mito, e del gioco dei tarocchi, Calvino demistifica la scienza concepita come ideologia . . . o come etica e teleologia . . . e propone invece quale fine dell'attività umana, quel "fare" tipicamente umano che è attribuzione di significato—[43]

> By the very fact that he puts science on the same footing as the fairytale, the myth and the Tarot game, Calvino demystifies the concept of science as ideology . . . or as ethics and teleology . . . and he proposes instead as the aim of human activity that typically human "doing" which is the attribution of meaning—

and proceeds to exemplify this demystification through an analysis of scientific language and "Qfwfq's discourse" in "La distanza della luna."

A. Illiano devotes several pages to the effects of demystification through humor in *Le cosmicomiche*, declaring that: "Calvino demistifica l'uomo catapultandolo con tutte le sue meschinità in un universo deformato da un ipolinguaggio antilirico" (Calvino demystifies man, catapulting him in all his pettiness into a universe deformed by an antilyrical hypolanguage)[44] and "Calvino riduce la vita stessa a un gioco astruso di possibilità legate al passato, a una serie di eventualità predeterminate da leggi generiche" (Calvino reduces life to an abstruse game of possiblities linked to the past, to a series of eventualities predetermined by generic laws).[45] Illiano feels that Calvino demystifies "il dinamismo moderno," "l'industrializzazione globale," and "il progresso tecnologico":

> Nell'area dell'impegno etico-ideologico si colloca anche la demitizzazione della scienza e dello scibile umano . . . A tratti la parodia raggiunge apici di ludicro divertimento barocco . . . che può sottintendere una radicale sfiducia nella scienza come metodo assoluto per comprendere la realtà e il bisogno di riconoscere alla letteratura e all'ingegno un maggior potere di comprensione e di conoscenza.[46]

> The demythicization of science and human knowledge is also situated in the area of ethical-ideological commitment . . . At points the parody reaches peaks of ludicrous baroque fun . . . that can imply a radical distrust of science as an absolute method of understanding reality and the need to recognize in literature and in ingenuity a greater capacity for understanding and knowledge.

Finally, Illiano feels that the creation of Qfwfq "sotto il velo della demitizzazione umoristica, ne ribadisce il fondamentale impegno ideologico" (under the veil of humorous demythicization reconfirms its fundamental ideological commitment).[47] Bernardini Napoletano also identifies humor as Calvino's primary tool for demystification and affirms the "impegno," the commitment, that motivates and underlies such techniques: "non resta allo scrittore che non voglia integrarsi [alla realtà] altra strada per demistificarla che quella aggirante della satira" (no other road for demystifying [reality] is left to the writer who does not want to become integrated into it but the roundabout one of satire).[48] She continues, further clarifying the connection between humor, demystification and "impegno,"

> Un nuovo impegno è possibile soltanto nell'accettazione della difficile posizione di "intellettuale inorganico" e nella pratica letteraria dello *humour* e dell'utopia, i quali rifiutano e mettono in crisi i moderni "miti dell'efficienza, del successo, del denaro": il *trait d'union* tra il polo letterario dell' *irrisione* e quello politico della *rivoluzione* è costituito proprio dalla dimensione ludica.[49]

> A new commitment is possible only in the acceptance of the difficult position of the "inorganic intellectual" and in the literary practice of *humor* and utopia, which refute and throw into crisis the modern "myths of efficiency, success and money": the *trait d'union* between the literary pole of *derision* and the political one of *revolution* is constituted precisely by the ludic dimension.

C. Milanini, in a recent article on the "realistic" *Trilogy* ("Speculazione," "Giornata" and "Smog"), continues this connection beween demystification and its underlying objective of "impegno":

> il realismo esistenziale dell'autore ligure è innervato da un forte intento demistificante, sottende un accanimento strenuo contro le più sottili forme di falsa coscienza . . . resta sempre operante l'impegno a smascherare gli inganni e gli autoinganni, i compromessi pratici e le pseudogiustificazioni ideali di un'umanità che ha soffocato in sé ogni autentica tensione etica per meglio godere del benessere materiale acquisito negli anni del "miracolo economico."[50]

> the existential realism of the Ligurian author is innervated by a strong demystifying intent, it subtends a bold obstinacy against the most subtle forms of false conscience . . . always in operation is the commitment to unmask deceptions and self-deceptions, the practical

compromises and the ideal pseudojustifications of a humankind that has suffocated within itself every authentic ethical tension in order to better enjoy the material well-being acquired in the years of the "economic miracle."

This last comment, which emphasizes the prevalence and purpose of Calvino's use of demystification, leads to one of our final observations. Discussion of the issue of Calvino's "impegno," his "engagement," his political or social involvement or commitment, constitutes perhaps the most important ongoing discussion on Calvino's work and literary philosophy, especially insofar as it embraces many other concerns and ideas, including some of those just addressed. However, it is far from a unifying trait from a critical standpoint. Critics have been struggling over, and disagreeing on, this crucial question from the beginning. In its complexity, the issue of *engagement* encompasses many concerns and has taken a multitude of forms over the years, as it evolved to match the literary concerns of each period. While a comprehensive look at this phenomenon in criticism of Calvino would be too intricate and vast an undertaking in the present context, it seems nonetheless essential, given its import, to expose a few of the most prominent currents in the polemic and to establish our own stance before initiating the investigation of eros in Calvino.

The discussion commences perhaps with Calvino's active participation as a young man in the Resistance with his brother; their activities implicated their anti-fascist parents, who were held in captivity while Calvino and his brother were hiding in the mountains. This experience—it is generally accepted—is reflected in his early *Racconti*. The portrayals of these experiences led the author, as well as his critics, to identify himself with the neorealist movement which, very broadly speaking, saw literature's function as deeply linked to social change, to the formation of a better Italy after the defeat of Fascism, and to issues regarding the rights of the lower classes. Intellectuals felt they had a responsibility to communicate with, and express, the plight of the poor, to become involved in exposing the corruption which subjugated them. These beliefs had various ramifications, linguistic as well as ideological, in art; simply speaking, the use of means of expression that could be immediately grasped by the downtrodden proletariat and the illiterate was advocated. These ideas coincided with the ideals of Italian communism, which was one of the forces behind the Resistance. Calvino was an active member of this party until 1957, and wrote for *l'Unità*, the Communist newspaper.

However, Calvino's ideas on the function of literature and its relation to politics and society did not coincide entirely with neorealist precepts. For example, Calvino felt that the experimentation with dialect (as a form of immediate communicability) was a sign of "involuzione e stanchezza" (involution and tiredness).[51] Nor did Calvino agree with the idea of literature as propaganda; he refuted the idea of the "mimesi pura e semplice delle organizzazioni di partito e delle Camere del Lavoro" (the pure and simple mimesis of party organizations and trade-union headquarters).[52] His split with the Communist party after it condoned Russia's invasion of Hungary was also significant in his mapping out a new role for literature; slowly he came to distance it from formal politics but not from political and social issues. Like many other intellectuals, he had suffered disillusionment about many unrealized post-war aspirations for his country and for the literary movement that grew out of these but that was now on the ebb. His feelings and the mood of the times can be gauged by his article, "Il midollo del leone" (1955), from which we have just quoted (now in *Una pietra sopra*).

Such distance from politics, a great disappointment to fellow Communist intellectuals, as one can imagine, coincided with another "betrayal" of post-war literary ideals: the publication of the novels which comprise his famous and by now classic trilogy *I nostri antenati* and which, compared to earlier more "realistic" works, are unmistakably fantastical. Although the critics had already begun to describe Calvino's earlier fiction as "favoloso" ("fairy-tale-like") Calvino shrewdly observes:

> Io stavo al gioco: capivo benissimo che il pregio è d'essere favolosi quando si parla di proletariato e di fattacci di cronaca, mentre a esserlo parlando di castelli e di cigni non c'è nessuna bravura.[53]

> I was willing to go along with it: I understood perfectly that the merit is in being fairy-tale-like when speaking of the proletariat and news about crime, while there is no skill in being so when speaking of castles and swans.

Needless to say, for years, accusations of "escapism" and "frivolity" clung to his works of fantasy, while some searched desperately for redeeming "meaning." Calvino remarked as regards *Il visconte*: "E i critici potevano cominciar ad andare su una falsa strada: dicendo che quel che mi stava a cuore era il problema del bene e del male" (And the critics could set out on the wrong road: saying that what really mattered to me was the issue of good and evil).[54]

As Barilli very accurately observed in a 1959 review of *I racconti,*

> Da quanto si è detto è facile comprendere che a Calvino riesce quanto mai difficile essere scrittore *engagé,* se per *engagement* intendiamo la dichiarata adesione a una ideologia valida al livello sociale, impegnativa per la prassi politica, volta a proporre una teleologia classista (questo è oggi purtroppo nel nostro ambiente culturale il senso che si dà al termine *engagement;* non si pensa che lo scrittore potrebbe essere *engagé* per il fatto di accettare un'epistemologia, una concezione psicologica piuttosto che un'altra, e che di conseguenza indice del suo impegno potrebbe essere la scelta di certi strumenti tecnici piuttosto che di altri).[55]

> From what has been said it is very easy to understand that for Calvino it is very difficult to be an *engagé* writer, if for *engagement* we mean the avowed adherence to an ideology that is valid on a social plane, binding in political praxis, devoted to proposing a class teleology (this is unfortunately in our cultural context the meaning that is given to the term *engagement;* it doesn't occur to us that the writer could be *engagé* in so far as he accepts one epistemology, one psychological concept, over another, and that consequently a gauge of his commitment might be his choosing certain literary devices rather than others).

Barilli goes on to say that "Calvino è stato in grado di entrare tra i primi in rottura col clima fittizio e pesante del nostro neorealismo postbellico" (Calvino was in a position to be amongst the first to break with the heavy and fictitious climate of our postwar neorealism).[56] Years later, in a 1968 review of Calvino's "scientific" creations, Barilli observed that the literary climate in Italy changed in Calvino's favor in the 1960s:

> Come ben si sa infatti è largamente caduta in discredito una nozione di impego di tipo ideologico, fondata su più o meno manifeste professioni di fede politica; e in corrispondenza di ciò è apparso del tutto logoro, ormai infrequentabile il ricorso a circostanze *vere,* documentarie, legate a precisi ambienti e contesti sociali.[57]

> As is well known, in fact, the notion of commitment of an ideological type, founded on more or less manifest professions of political faith, has largely fallen into disrepute; and along the same lines, the recourse to *real* circumstances—documented, linked to specific

social contexts and environments—has shown itself to be entirely worn out, and by now no longer an option.

However, Woodhouse's contemporaneous analysis (1968) and defense of the trilogy *I nostri antenati* indicate that accusations of escapism still clung to Calvino's works of fantasy.[58] The discourse at this point assumes yet another form, becoming an investigation, which is still ongoing, of the purpose and validity of works of fantasy, as is much of Calvino's output in the sixties and early seventies, as well as the fifties. An indication that fantasy to some extent still equaled escapism is Heiney's fine 1968 article, which begins almost with an apology of fantasy. He refutes the imputation that the modern tendency toward fantasy is equivalent to a thrust toward escapism and asserts that it is rather a dissatisfaction with the present fictional conventions that deal with the world, and not a dissatisfaction with the world itself.[59] That misconceptions of fantasy still persist is evidenced by the fact that Calvino himself obliquely refers to this issue in the posthumously published *Six Memos for the Next Millennium*, only five of which were completed. (Calvino died before he could present these "lezioni" for the prestigious Charles E. Norton Lecture series at Harvard University.) "Leggerezza" (lightness) is the title of his first lecture. His reference to "la letteratura come funzione esistenziale, la ricerca della leggerezza come reazione al peso di vivere" (literature as an existential function, the search for lightness as a reaction to the weight of living) denotes the significance of the continuation of the debate over fantasy versus escapism.[60] Calvino says,

Alla precarietà dell'esistenza della tribù,—siccità, malattie, influssi maligni—lo sciamano rispondeva annullando il peso del suo corpo, trasportandosi in volo in un altro mondo, in un altro livello di percezione, dove poteva trovare le forze per modificare la realtà ... Credo che sia una costante antropologica questo nesso tra levitazione desiderata e privazione sofferta. E'questo dispositivo antropologico che la letteratura perpetua.

Faced with the precarious existence of tribal life—drought, sickness, evil influences—the shaman responded by ridding his body of weight and flying to another world, another level of perception, where he could find the strength to change the face of reality ... I find it a steady feature in anthropology, this link between the levitation desired and the privation actually suffered. It is this anthropological device that literature perpetuates.[61]

Calvino seems in this way to be countering any attempts to insist that fantastical literature must be unequivocally meaningless.

But accusations of having produced "meaningless" fiction, which had been leveled at Calvino during his departure from neorealism, arose yet again in a new form, or at least with a different basis, when Calvino began to manifestly incorporate modern literary critical theories in his narratives. *Il castello* and *Se una notte* are the two most obvious examples of this, but some of *Le cosmicomiche* also reveal his manipulation of such contemporary theories as structuralism, semiotics, and other metanarrative theories on methods of artistic creation and interpretation. Many believed that in his creative pursuits, which now involved utilizing the theories of self-referentiality mentioned above, Calvino had ceased to believe that literature could say anything significant about reality, society or humanity. Perhaps this logically resulted—to oversimplify the intricate, evolving discourse on the plight of contemporary literature—because semiotics, for example, limits words to the function of a sign, the mere function of a sign, one could say, which can in no way represent reality. Modern literary criticism has exploded the connection between the sign and its signified; it has laid bare the arbitrariness of the relation. Thus modern literature's crisis, mentioned briefly above, is manifested by its obsession with itself. Its self-reflexivity is a prime example of its inability to say anything beyond itself, to know anything beyond itself, to have meaning.

At the present time, many critics are divided on how to interpret Calvino's use, in *Il castello*, *Le città invisibili*, *Palomar*, and especially in the most experimental work, *Se una notte*, of metanarrative, metaliterary technique and ideology. As noted in our discussion of demystification, L. Guj, Bernardini Napoletano, Illiano, and R. Andrews, just to name a few, directly or indirectly depict Calvino as *engagé*—though no longer in the strictly political sense. They see him as a firm believer in the meaning of literature and in literature's ability to give meaning to the world and to "teach," in the broadest sense. De Lauretis recognizes in Calvino's work both a tendency to promote action as well as contemplation and artistic creation. She convincingly

argue[s] that ... Calvino's works remain constantly focused on a basic vision of human activity as both praxis and poesis, and that, if thematic polarity does exist in his narrative, it is not a contradictory impasse but rather a dialectic process reflecting his awareness of the very nature of culture as the highest and unique form of human "doing."[62]

Cannon, on the other hand, feels that Calvino, starting as far back as *I nostri antenati*, began to doubt literature's ability to reach outside itself, to teach, to express or give meaning.[63]

A look at Calvino's own comments on the function of literature, or rather on literature's potential to have a valid function— surely a pivotal and all-encompassing concern for any writer— might be illuminating. Bruscagli, in an article on *Una pietra sopra* called "Autobiografia (perplessa) di Italo Calvino" which captures the elusive nature of Calvino's collection of essays, summarizes Calvino's significant concluding article thus:

> L'ultimo intervento (*I livelli della realtà in letteratura*, 1978), arrivando a concludere che la letteratura non tanto conosce i livelli della realtà quanto la realtà dei suoi livelli, dei suoi interni piani di costruzione, chiude l'itinerario in un ribadimento ormai irreversibile di coatta, per quanto scaltrissima, autonomia.[64]

> The last essay ("I livelli della realtà in letteratura," 1978), reaching the conclusion that literature does not so much know the levels of reality as the reality of its levels, of its own internal structure, concludes the itinerary in a by-now irreversible confirmation of a compulsory, though very sly, autonomy.

However, in light of the preface to this collection of essays, Bruscagli wisely inquires, "A libro chiuso, è inevitabile chiedersi quanto l'itinerario del romanzo critico si identifichi e quanto si distacchi rispetto a quello del Calvino romanziere" (With the book snapped shut, we inevitably ask ourselves how much the itinerary of the critical novel coincides with and how much it diverges from the itinerary of Calvino the novelist)[65] and concludes his article with another crucial question: "Ce la farà ad attraversare, stavolta, il gran mare della teoria della letteratura?" (Will he manage, this time, to cross the great sea of literary theory?).[66]

While this concluding article to *Una pietra sopra* seems undoubtedly to limit literature to knowledge of itself, one must remember that it is merely another in a series of articles Calvino has "done with"—"sopra cui ha messo una pietra." To this concluding article, we would like to juxtapose the initial article, one of Calvino's most often-quoted pieces, "Il midollo del leone." The following excerpt is perhaps one of his most renowned af-

firmations: "Noi pure siamo tra quelli che credono in una letteratura come educazione, di grado e di qualità insostituibili" (We
are also among those who believe in a literature as education, of
an irreplaceable grade and quality).[67] He goes on to say, "In ogni
vera poesia, esiste . . . un nutrimento per una morale rigorosa"
(In every real poem, there is . . . nourishment for rigorous morals).[68] Toward the end he affirms:

> Non sono la decadenza, l'irrazionalità, la crudeltà, la corsa alla morte
> dell'arte e della letteratura che devono farci paura; sono la de-
> cadenza, l'irrazionalità, la crudeltà, la corsa alla morte che leggiamo
> continuamente nella vita degli uomini e dei popoli, e di cui l'arte e
> la letteratura ci possono fare coscienti e forse immuni, ci possono
> indicare la trincea morale in cui difenderci.[69]

> It is not the decadence, the irrationality, the cruelty, the headlong
> rush toward death of art and literature that should frighten us; it is
> rather the decadence, the irrationality, the cruelty, the headlong rush
> toward death that we continuously read about in the lives of men
> and of the peoples, of which art and literature can make us aware
> and maybe immune. They can show us the moral trench in which
> to defend ourselves.

While this article struggles beneath its "pietra," it merits attention because the idea of "morale" continues to appear in Calvino's essays as a sort of personal ideal right until the end of his
life. For example, Calvino ends his article, "La sfida al labirinto"
(1962) by upholding his "continua esigenza . . . di giudizi mo-
rali": "che anche di ciò che ora si rifiuta (e forse ha le sue ragioni
per rifiutarsi) a un giudizio morale, quel che conta per noi è
quello che ci insegna" (continuous demand . . . for moral judg-
ments: even what now refuses (and maybe it has its reasons for
refusing) to submit to a moral judgment, what counts for us is
what it teaches us).[70] Calvino also discusses "la morale" in relation to Il barone in his introduction to the 1965 edition, under
the heading, "La ricerca di una morale."[71] This view of literature
as instruction, as expressing values, might also be at the root of
Calvino's many children's editions, as well as his many introductions to his texts. Calvino himself refers to this notion of "morale" as his unchanging ideal, in one of his very last interviews
before his death, the interview he granted to Maria Corti:

> All'epoca in cui ho cominciato a pormi il problema di come scrivere,
> cioè nei primi anni Quaranta, c'era un'idea di morale che doveva dar

forma allo stile, e questo è forse ciò che più mi è rimasto, di quel
clima della letteratura italiana d'allora, attraverso tutta la distanza
che ci separa.[72]

At the time I began to consider the problem of how to write, that is,
in the early 1940s, there was an idea of *moral* that was to give shape
to one's style, and this is perhaps what has remained with me most
from the climate of Italian literature back then, over all the distance
that separates us.

While this idea of "morale" seems to be the self-proclaimed
nucleus of Calvino's writing, the term remains tantalizingly ambiguous throughout his writings. It would, however, be a misin-
terpretation to interpret Calvino's idea of "morale" in any
narrow, limiting, or dogmatic sense of the word. Nothing in Calvino's writing leads us to believe that he is referring to religious
or other institutionalized "moral codes"; he creates his own. The
type of "morale" which has informed much of his writing seems
to refer to his contribution as a writer to the social problems or
concerns of the times, so that "morale" becomes inextricably
intertwined with his "stile" (his choice of protagonist, voice, language, etc.). For example, in *Il barone rampante*, the moral Calvino may be advocating may be a staunch individuality and the
critical distance necessary to understand one's society, with Cosimo as the paradigm of such an ideal. In *Le cosmicomiche*, the
moral may be what Calvino expressed in an interview:

He [Qfwfq] is more than anything a voice or a pair of eyes, a pair of
human eyes, a kind of anthropomorphization of a biological creature.
    I tried to do for modern science what primitive people have done
with the forces of nature: personify them with figures between the
human and the animal. These stories are the legends and the myths
of the world of science.[73]

Calvino has been committed throughout his writing career to
presenting his ideals in new and impactive ways (using, as many
have noted, the technique of "straniamento"). A critic who has
given perhaps the most sensitive and exhaustive reading of Calvino's "moral" commitments as a writer is Vittorio Spinazzola in
his ambitious article, "L'io diviso di Italo Calvino." The following
passage is an example of this critic's contributions:

Come letterato e come intellettuale, Calvino apprezzò positivamente
l'opportunità di allargare e approfondire il rapporto non solo con

l'utenza libraria ma con l'opinione pubblica più vasta. Capì infatti
che ciò non implicava alcuna necessità invincibile di adeguamento
al conformismo, anzi esaltava l'atteggiamento di responsabilità auto-
noma di chi vuole e sa orientare le idee correnti, non facendosene
condizionare . . . Gli è che per Calvino era impensabile assumere le
pose solenne del vate e del profeta, sicuro delle verità infallibili da
esibire a chi lo legga o lo ascolti. Il suo temperamento lo chiamava
a scegliersi la parte dell'educatore di massa, intento a persuadere la
coscienza comune della complessità dei problemi che volta a volta
lo agitano.[74]

As a man of letters and as an intellectual, Calvino judged the opportunity to widen and deepen the relationship not only with book
users but with wider public opinion a positive thing. He understood
in fact that this did not imply any unconquerable necessity to adapt
to conformism; rather it exalted an attitude of autonomous responsibility of one who wants and knows how to direct current ideas,
without allowing himself to be conditioned by them . . . So it is that
for Calvino it was unthinkable to strike the solemn poses of a bard
and prophet, certain of the infallible truths to be imparted to those
who might read or listen to him. His temperament required him to
choose the role of educator of the masses, intent on persuading the
common conscience of the complexity of the problems that from
time to time upset him.

Thus the recurrence of "morale" in Calvino's essays, interviews, and introductions certainly cannot be ignored, and indicates the validity of a fundamental precept that has stayed with
Calvino, according to the Corti interview, from beginning to end.
The following quote, coincidentally from another interview
given in 1985, strikes us as another example of Calvino's revindi-
cation of literature's importance in society:

What hasn't changed is what I demand of a book that I write. I want
to have a relationship with the reader. I want the reader to have fun.
I don't want to be a boring writer. At the same time, *I want my books
to have a meaning and to have a meaning in the culture of our times;*
to say something that hasn't already been said and to say it in a way
that cannot be said except through literature. I believe more and
more in literature as a language that says things that the other languages can't say, that literature has full status as a form of knowledge.[75] (Italics mine)

These, as his last interviews, warrant special attention and
attain a certain prominence and finality. They reflect some of
Calvino's last thoughts on, and perceptions of, literature, its func-

tion, its meaning—and its ability to generate meaning. We can therefore understand Calvino not only as a complex, innovative, ironic, and provocative figure, but also as uniquely engagé.

It would not be amiss here to mention one of the most widely recognized influences on Calvino's style and theory of literature, one he has often acknowledged: the French Age of Enlightenment. His proclivity for fantasy, his advocacy of an instructional literature (however undidactic), as well as his marked interest in rationalism and science, can be traced back, at least in part, to his continued fascination with, and interest in, the literature of the Enlightenment. This influence has also contributed to Calvino's insistence on *clarity* of expression.[76] Gardair asserts:

> Fonte inesauribile di modelli conoscitivi e di vita associativa, fonte soprattutto di una cultura in cui teoria e prassi si condizionano e si verificano a vicenda, il Settecento francese riassume senz'altro *in nuce* le varie forme dell'opera e dell'operare calviniano finora indagate.[77]

> An inexhaustible source of cognitive models and interactive life, a source above all of a culture in which theory and praxis condition and verify each other reciprocally, the French eighteenth century summarizes without a doubt, *in nuce*, the various forms of Calvino's work and methods of working studied up to now.

Without investigating these eighteenth-century roots further, we would like to mention a few studies done in this vein. For example, Gardair explores, as many have done, the relation between *Il barone rampante*, set in the 1700s in Italy, and the Enlightenment period in France, and then traces this novel's connection with Diderot. In another study, Bryce cites Calvino's continued fascination with the eighteenth century ("proprio perché lo scopro sempre più ricco, sfaccettato, pieno di fermenti contraddittori che continuano fino ad oggi" [precisely because I discover it to be always richer, more multifaceted, full of contradictory ferment that continues to the present day]) and embarks on a comparison of the works of Rousseau and *Il barone*.[78]

Having prepared the groundwork, let us now proceed to the central topic of this study, a topic to which critics have been, in view of the abundant studies on Calvino, relatively inattentive: *the role of eros in Calvino's fiction*. We will investigate this from a linguistic as well as thematic perspective, and try to evaluate the weight and function of its role in his texts. While our discussion will not focus specifically on the relationship of the constants of "contrast," games, and demystification with eros, some connections will surface during the course of our study, since these elements pervade his work. However, we will conclude our study with the intriguing connection between literature's ability to represent reality and to give meaning, and erotic love as Calvino portrays it in a text published posthumously, *Sotto il sole giaguaro*. First, however, it behooves us to ascertain the weight eros has in his texts, and to fathom a reason for the relative silence of the critics.

2

An Evolving Theory on
the Language of Love

A neglected theme: What the critics do and don't say

In her 1984 dissertation on the theme of romantic love in Calvino's fiction—a study which stresses love's prevalence in his texts and briefly explores its connection with creativity and metanarrative—Miriam Friedman writes, "One . . . traditional theme, found to recur over and over again in Calvino, is the theme of love. Although it often has a very prominent place in his stories, its presence has been overlooked and even denied by critics."[1] Since 1984, there has been a great deal of research on sundry angles of Calvino's thought and writings, from studies of his newspaper contributions, to his variants, to his collaboration with musical texts, to his connections with optics and astronomy (to name just a few of the topics that have drawn attention outside of the still-debated topics of fantasy versus realism, fable and fairy tale, the function of *ars combinatoria*, and metanarrative critical methodologies, etc.). Amidst this avalanche of impassioned exploration, Friedman's words still hold for the most part true. Several collections of articles presented at conferences in honor of Calvino, for example, have had barely a word to say about eros in his fiction.[2]

The exceptions to this silence concern the two texts that *have* commanded studies on love, perhaps because the stories depend on romantic plot movement: *Le cosmicomiche* and *Se una notte*. In the former, seventeen out of twenty-five stories (not including the four *Ti con zero* stories) are constructed around romantic entanglements.[3] Perhaps fiction writer Michael Stephens best succeeds in underscoring the erotic impact of this collection (and of *Le città invisibili*). He transmits the sensual ambience of Calvino's world, where eros is personified—within recognizably traditional dictates—as woman, where the impossible is not only probable, but a possibility of great unattainable fulfillment, the naked woman in the Moon, the woman of Khan's city, naked and long-haired, or with firm nipples pushing against you. It is comic, it is like a comic strip, where the women have those lush figures like Winnie Winkle and Brenda Starr, like Wonder Woman and Veronica . . . I see a beautiful woman coming toward me on a street in the invisible city, and all the street lights are a buttery light like the Moon's.[4]

In the second text to draw analyses of love, *Se una notte*, love and reading, as many scholars have observed, run a parallel course and often become intertwined in the main plotline; in addition, a love story always propels the *incipits*. Mary McCarthy provocatively interprets even Calvino's relation to the reader as erotic; she feels both are involved in "un juego amoroso" (a love game), and sees the ten *incipits* as moments of "coitus interruptus."[5] Albert Carter feels *Se una notte* is "Calvino's most erotic book."[6] Segre underlines "la forte emergenza dell'eros" (the strong emergence of eros) in *Se una notte*, but adds: "quell'eros che finora, mi pare, costituiva un'apparizione molto rara nei suoi scritti" (that eros that, until now, it seems to me, constituted a very rare appearance in his writings).[7] That this last opinion might be tendered by many other scholars is evident by their silence on the topic of eros in Calvino's other fictions, or their rather cursory glance at it.

Besides Friedman's, very few studies attempt an intertextual exploration of love; one that does is Marilyn Schneider's "Calvino's Erotic Metaphor and the Hermaphroditic Solution."[8] Friedman points out, however, that, ironically, Schneider feels "Calvino's fiction is relatively inattentive to romantic love"[9]— "notwithstanding its erotic element."[10] The rest of Schneider's comment, which merits some discussion, is as follows:

> Where he introduces a love element, it functions ultimately to elaborate a quest for wholeness rather than to develop a love story. The erotic relationships illustrate the tensions of desire as an internal psychic force and as a way of perceiving reality. They also allegorize the writer's relationship to his writing. In short, the sexual factor is broadly metaphoric and mythic.[11]

While Calvino undoubtedly utilizes love relationships in the manner which Schneider describes, i.e., as reflections of internal struggle and other thematic concerns, so do many writers, even those who "develop a love story," to use Schneider's words. The loved one, or the erotic quest itself, usually provides an opportunity as a device with which the writer can shed light on the personality, goals, fears, etc., of the protagonist. Often, the loved one functions as an alter ego. So Calvino is not unique in this use of love relationships.

In addition, Calvino, contrary to Schneider's belief, does at some points "develop a love story," and most notably in *Il barone rampante*, which is a fine comment on the friction between two incompatible individuals in love. *Se una notte* also traces the anguish and awe of the *Lettore's* fascination with the *Lettrice*, which not only has (as has been noted) metaphoric value, but also reveals Calvino's sensitivity to the trials and satisfactions of romantic love and his attempt to present them in original ways. So do the "slices of love stories" of *Gli amori difficili*. The story "Sotto il sole giaguaro," published after Schneider's article appeared, offers another significant insight into cohabitation (or conjugal life, as the case may be).

Eros, defined in Calvino's fictions as heterosexual love with roots, for the most part, in the tradition of pursuit of the desired object (usually—but not always—a pursuit of the female by the male), appears as far back as *Il sentiero* and the soldiers' associations with Pin's sister. Eros impels each story of *I nostri antenati* forward and plays an important part in the "realistic" trilogy. It is the central theme of *Gli amori difficili* and occurs in *Il castello* and even tangentially in *Le città*. Eros is fundamental to *Le cosmicomiche*, to *Se una notte*, and to *Sotto il sole giaguaro*, a posthumously published text which has only begun to receive attention and includes the eponymous short story mentioned above.

Why, then, are not more scholars talking about it? Why is it handled almost as an "aside" that is not relevant to the topics at hand? There may be at least two reasons why this is so. First, the theme of love in Calvino seems to be considered self-evident, and characterized for the most part by pursuit, absence and lack of communication between characters. De Lauretis, in her comment on "L'avventura di un viaggiatore" from *Gli amori difficili*, observes,

> This core of silence at the bottom of human communication is an area of passivity, a non-disposable residue of negativity that, for Calvino, is the essence of the sexual relationship. Desire is founded in absence, in the tension-toward rather than the attainment of the object of love, in the delays, the displacements, the deferrals.[12]

Another example of this type of definition of love in Calvino comes from S. M. Adler:

Many of Calvino's stories deal with love relationships. Yet, more often than not, the author is concerned with a particular kind of love: love which regards couples who are somehow separated from each other, the relationship that becomes a struggle and a test because of "*absence.*" Once again, therefore, it may be said that Calvino's stories about love hold a striking resemblance to Italian fables ... The love one finds in fables, explains Calvino, is always "precarious love," the love "that meets its test in absence."[13]

Earlier, Adler had observed, in a section entitled "Unfulfilled desires": "More often that not ... the characters affected by frustrating desires are lovers."[14] "Stories about lovers who do not meet are to be found everywhere in Calvino's narrative," Adler confirms and proceeds to list examples from *Il cavaliere*, *Il barone* and "Il guidatore notturno" in the 1970 edition of *Gli amori difficili.*[15]

These perfectly accurate comments do in a sense capture the character of love relations in Calvino, but there is more that needs to be said. Desire, pursuit and unattainability, absence and lack of communication are familiar catchall words that conceal deeper layers of meaning worth exploring. Thus far, they have rather represented where the discussion stops.

An early theory on the language of love

The second reason for the inattentiveness to eros in Calvino's works may have its roots in the language that he chooses to represent the erotic. His choices are grounded, as we will see, in his theories on eroticism in literature. There seem to be no studies on the language of love in Calvino—that is, on the language he uses to portray lovers, their sexual and romantic feelings and encounters, and on the place he considers eroticism and love should occupy in literature. Perhaps this is where our investigation should begin.

There is no doubt whatsoever that language is of prime consideration to a painstaking, sophisticated writer—and editor!—such as Calvino is. We mentioned earlier two studies, one by Bernardini Napoletano and the other by De Lauretis, on the linguistic innovations and contrasts in *Le cosmicomiche*. In addition, at the 1987 conference in Florence on Calvino, Pier Vincenzo Mengaldo presented a superb paper called, "Il linguaggio dello scrittore," a paper which has recently become available. (We will refer to it later in our discussion of *Le cosmicomiche*.)[16]

Calvino himself reiterated the importance of language, and especially *precision* in language, in articles and interviews, demonstrating in commentary the attention to language his fiction reveals. Calvino's concern with, and focus on, language can be traced from his earlier essays through some of his last interviews, and forms a veritable linguistic theory. As far back as 1956, in his famous "Il midollo del leone," Calvino rejected the contemporary interest in writing in dialect. Vittorio Colletti, who explores Calvino's interest in a *precise* Italian and his exemplification of it, quotes him as saying,

> La lingua letteraria deve sì continuamente tenersi attenta ai volgari parlati, e nutrirsene e rinnovarsene, ma non deve annullarsi in essi, né scimmiottarli per gioco. Lo scrittore deve poter dire più cose di quelle che normalmente dicono gli uomini del suo tempo: deve costruirsi una lingua la più complessa e funzionale possibile per il proprio tempo.[17]

> Literary language must certainly stay continuously attuned to spoken languages, and nourish and renew itself on them, but it must not vanish within them, nor mimic them for play. The writer must be able to say more things than the men of his time would normally say: he must build for himself as complex and functional a language as possible for his time.

About a decade after he wrote this article, i.e., at about the same time he published the first edition of *Le cosmicomiche*, Calvino penned several articles, now also in *Una pietra*, in the debate on the Italian language instigated by Pasolini's definition of the new "technological" Italian. In these articles, which position Italian not in contrast to dialects (as before) but to other national languages, especially as regards issues of "translatability" and the modern Italian language's ability to communicate, Calvino rejects "i vizi di cent'anni di burocratizzazione dell'italiano" (the bad habits of a hundered years of bureaucratization of Italian).[18] He rejects "il linguaggio 'obiettivo'" of TV news when it summarizes the talks of political leaders: "tutti ridotti a minime variazioni della stessa combinazione di termini anodini, incolori e insapori" (all reduced to slight variations of the same combinations of anodynic, dull, flavorless terms).[19] He continues his attacks in "Antilingua," the second article from this period:

> Avvocati e funzionari, gabinetti ministeriali e consigli d'amministrazione, redazioni di giornali e di telegiornali scrivono parlano pensano nell'antilingua. Caratteristica principale dell'antilingua è

quello che definirei il "terrore semantico," cioè la fuga di fronte a
ogni vocabolo che abbia di per se stesso un significato, come se "fia-
sco" "stufa" "carbone" fossero parole oscene, come se "andare" "trovare" "sapere" indicassero azioni turpi.[20]

Lawyers and public officials, cabinets and boards of directors, newspaper and television news editorial staff write, speak and think in
the antilanguage. The principal characteristic of the antilanguage is
what I would define as "semantic terror," that is, a flight in the face
of any word that has, in and of itself, a meaning, as if "flask," "oven"
and "coal" were obscene words, as if "going," "finding" and "know-
ing" indicated filthy actions.

The scathing sarcasm of his final examples transmits the strength
of his convictions. Calvino's ideal of language as "concreto" and
"preciso," his opposition to "espressioni astratte e generiche"
was reiterated in two recent interviews.[21] In 1981, Calvino gave,
as one of three talismen for the year 2000, "combattere l'astrat-
tezza del linguaggio che ci viene imposta ormai da tutte le parti.
Puntare sulla precisione, tanto nel linguaggio quanto nelle cose
che si fanno" (to combat the vagueness of language that by now
is imposed on us from all sides. To aim for precision, as much
in language as in the things we do).[22] In the 1985 interview with
Maria Corti, he responded as follows to her question on the
"identity" of his language: "Posso solo dire che cerco di oppormi
alla pigrizia mentale di cui danno prova tanti miei colleghi ro-
manzieri nel loro uso d'un linguaggio quanto mai prevedibile e
insipido" (I can only say that I try to oppose the mental laziness
that so many of my novelist colleagues display in their use of a
language that is predictable and insipid in the extreme).[23] Again,
in his Six Memos, under "Esattezza," Calvino includes language,
"un linguaggio il più preciso possible come lessico e come resa
delle sfumature del pensiero e dell'immaginazione" (a language
as precise as possible both in choice of words and in expression
of the subtleties of thought and imagination).[24] Such consistent
reaffirmation of his earliest convictions highlights both the emphasis Calvino places on precision as fundamental to all types
of language—literary, legal, technical, journalistic, specialized,
and everyday language—and the care he devotes to his own linguistic and semantic choices.

Calvino's linguistic theories are particularly significant to our
discussion on eros, especially in relation to an essay by Calvino
on eroticism and erotic language in literature. This essay, published in 1961, directly contradicts Calvino's convictions on pre-

cise language. The essay was Calvino's contribution to the issue
"Otto domande sull'erotismo in letteratura," in *Nuovi argomenti*
and may explain a certain lack of explicitly erotic language, especially in Calvino's fiction preceding the essay.[25] The ideas it ex-
pounds may also in part account for the near-vacuum of
scholarly interest in love in Calvino.

Most striking in this relatively little-known article is the caustic tone and the extremist position taken by our author, an otherwise very cautious intellectual whose "perplessità sistematica"
prevents him from taking even himself seriously.[26] The relative
obscurity of this article is perhaps due to the fact that Calvino
did not include it in *Una pietra*, although in his brief but complex article, "Il sesso e il riso," (1969), which we will discuss in
the following section and which was included in *Una pietra*, he
refers to it in a footnote. He seems, eight years later, to mitigate
the harshness of the tone of the previous article and his sternly
uncompromising views; he explains: "un partito preso di con-
traddizione verso Moravia, direttore della rivista, mi portava a
estremizzare la mia tesi in una sottovalutazione sistematica della
rappresentazione diretta della sessualità" (a position taken in
contradiction to Moravia, director of the journal, led me to carry
my theory to the extreme of systematically underrating the direct
representation of sexuality).[27]

Let's turn to the early article itself, which begins with a pro-
nouncement whose tone hints at the harshness to come: "Al
sesso i contemporanei pensano ancora troppo. Chi ci pensa
troppo non è libero" (My contemporaries still think too much
about sex. Whoever thinks too much about it is not free—Calvino, "Otto domande," p. 21). Calvino goes on to say that although the sexual repression affected by religious morality is on
the decline, it is being replaced by a conception of sex in "mythi-
cal" and "abstract" terms that merely constitutes another form
of "alienation." Calvino is probably alluding here to humanity's
alienation from nature, from one's own nature of which sex is
an integral part, almost in the Boccaccian sense. Calvino says he
feels "siamo più lontani che mai da una felicità naturale" (we
are farther than ever from a natural happiness—p. 21). It seems
in fact that Calvino feels that sex has not taken its rightful place
in the scale of social values and mores, as a natural force that
should neither be repressed nor exalted. He refuses both the conception of eroticism as "paradiso" and as "inferno":

Se in una società dominata da tabù e pregiudizi e rigorismi, il sesso era stato per la letteratura un grande simbolo di conoscenza, di contatto con la realtà, di verifica esistenziale, nel nostro secolo forse un solo autore: Hemingway, è riuscito ad affermare, in termini moderni, questo ordine di valori. (P. 21)

If in a society dominated by taboos and prejudices and rigorisms, sex had been for literature a great symbol of knowledge, of contact with reality, of existential verification, in our century, perhaps one author alone—Hemingway—has succeeded in affirming, in modern terms, this order of values.

Calvino then goes on to denounce the "rinnovato interesse erotico" (renewed erotic interest) in some Soviet novels, which he feels will in no way improve the quality of that country's literature, as well as America's naïveté in feeling it is still fighting Puritan values, and France's mix of philosophy and sex in place of the longstanding mix of theology and sex. "È sempre la stessa contaminazione di distinti che non può dare buoni frutti" (It is always the same contamination of distinct things which cannot produce good results—p. 22). He then observes, using the current issue of censorship in Italy, that censors and censured are both on the same side and their battle is a fake one because both are trying to reaffirm that "l'umanità è peccato e l'importante è preoccuparsi di questo peccato" (Humankind is sin and the important thing is to concern oneself with this sin—p. 22). Calvino has often spoken of his own secular education, of the fact that his parents insisted he be exempted from religious education. This further explains his intolerance of such religious repression (as "La giornata di uno scrutatore" also confirms) and his impatience with the dictates of such dogma.[28]

The answer, Calvino affirms throughout this article, is not to include eroticism in literature at all, because there is no way to weave it in assigning it its due place. "Un tedio mortale allunga la sua ombra sulla stessa parola 'erotismo' e su tutti i suoi riflessi in letteratura, nel cinema e sui giornali" (A deadly tedium throws its shadow on the very word "eroticism" and on all its reflections in literature, film and newspapers—Calvino, "Otto domande," p. 23). Significantly, this conclusion is one of only two sentences in the article that comprise a paragraph. Obviously, the brevity of these two paragraphs in relation to the longer paragraphs in the article underlines the emotional intensity of Calvino's pronouncements. The second short paragraph reads: "Per ora, tutto quello che possiamo dire è che nel Novecento l'erotismo non è un motivo poetico. Il nostro è il secolo"—and here he names one of his favorite authors—"di Kafka, scrittore casto" (For now, all we can say is that in the twentieth-century eroticism is not a poetic motif. Ours is the century—of Kafka, the chaste writer—p. 22).

In fact, he observes that the only ones who do manage to write about sex with "forza poetica" are those who consider it "torcendosi sdegnosamente il naso" (disdainfully wrinkling their noses). This certainly summarizes a strain, still strong in contemporary literature, to view sex negatively. This often testifies more to an aesthetic problem, i.e., the inability to write about it positively, to proclaim it a positive force without falling into cliché, than to moral inhibitions. Calvino goes on: "per chi si trova a considerare i rapporti amorosi con simpatia e gratitudine non resta che evitare di scriverne" (there's nothing for one who finds himself regarding love relations with liking and gratitude but to avoid writing about them—p. 21), and one feels that he numbers himself among these last. He seems to be affirming his positive view of human sexuality and at the same time underlining his own reluctance, or inability, to express such a view. "Ma forse è pur giusto così: chi è amico del sesso nella vita non può essere amico del sesso nella letteratura" (But perhaps this is only right: he who is a friend of sex in life cannot be a friend of sex in literature—p. 23). Calvino here seems to be denouncing the portrayal of sex as an "unhealthy" or "distorted" aspect of human life, and at the same time stating his own positive associations with sex. However, he also points to the irony that this positive view is sadly absent in literature. He says there are very few cases in which the image of a sexual encounter in fact is not "indegna di quel che esso è nella vita" (in some way unworthy of what it is in life—p. 23).

These last statements seem to amount to a sort of poetics of eroticism, which Calvino upheld and to some extent put into practice during at least the earlier years, the fifties, although parts of this theory, overstated in the article, reappear—as we will see in the following section—in later works. Calvino seems to be saying that sex, eros, romantic love, love relationships thwart and defy literature's representational abilities. They cannot be positively represented at least partly because of modern society's continuing confusion about sex and the constant swing between a vision of sex as "inferno" and a vision of it as "paradiso."

Unexpectedly, surprisingly—paradoxically!—our author, who advocates linguistic precision in all other instances, recommends silence in the realm of the sexual, and discourages detail. This is his "moral option," one might say, within the framework of his social and aesthetic considerations and discourse at the time. "Moral," however, must not be interpreted as that narrow view of ethical issues that derives from institutionalized dogma, such as religious or political dogma, for Calvino has never accepted a ready-made system of values. Nor does he appear to choose this option out of repulsion to sexual detail. Rather, the recommendation of silence seems to constitute Calvino's reaction to the problematic of representing the erotic positively. While aspects of this theory persist and develop into a more complex and mature theory in "Il sesso e il riso," they are here expressed unequivocally and uncompromisingly. Calvino refers to a few successful attempts to render the erotic in literature:

> Sono rari i casi—pagine soprattutto d'autori antichi e più che pagine brevi passi, veloci accordi di parole e di silenzi—in cui l'immagine del rapporto fisico sia in qualche modo non indegna di quel che esso è nella vita. (P. 23)

> The instances are rare—pages, above all, of ancient authors and not so much pages as brief passages, rapid combinations of words and silences—in which the image of a physical relationship is in some way not unworthy of what it is in life.

He goes on to applaud what his expression "veloci accordi di parole e di silenzi" already hints at: the poetic rendering of the erotic force. "Oggi che le immagini e le parole dell' 'erotismo' sono ormai logore e inservibili, resta all'espressione poetica l'infinita libertà dei traslati" (Today, with the images and the words of 'eroticism' by now worn and useless, poetic expresion is left with the infinite liberty of the metaphor—p. 24). Only poetic imagery can communicate the impact, the positive force, that eros has—or should have—in life. Calvino cites Dylan Thomas's chaste images and words as transmitting the strongest, most unmistakable "cariche di eros espresse nel nostro secolo" (erotic charges expressed in our century) and Borges's cosmic love as having far more emotional power than "la solita via della mimesi decadentistica delle sensazioni" (the usual route of the decadent mimesis of sensations—p. 24). It is noteworthy that Calvino quotes these passages on Thomas and Borges in a footnote in his

later article, suggesting at least one continuity perhaps in his
train of thought between 1961 and 1969.

The earlier article ends with Calvino's position, not only as
writer but as editor for Einaudi, clearly defined in the type of
letter he says he sends to young writers who send him their
manuscripts for assessment. The segment of the letter, almost
comic in severity, is worth reproducing:

> Egregio signore, ho esaminato il suo manoscritto, constatando che
> esso contiene passaggi di argomento erotico. Nel rimandarglielo per
> plico raccomandato, mi permetto di consigliarle d'espungere da esso
> tali passaggi e così ogni rappresentazione o menzione o allusione in
> materia e a voler evitare nelle sue opere future ogni riferimento a
> questi argomenti. (P. 24)

> Dear Sir, I have examined your manuscript, ascertaining that it con-
> tains passages of an erotic nature. In returning it to you by registered
> mail, I will take the liberty of advising you to expunge such passages
> from it and thus every representation or mention or allusion to the
> subject and to avoid in your future works any reference to these
> issues.

Theory and practice

How far can these views be verified in Calvino's own fictions
preceding and immediately surrounding the time of the article's
publication? Falaschi's philological investigations into the variants between the 1949 publication of *Ultimo viene il corvo* and
the 1958 edition of *I racconti* show editing decisions which cor-
roborate Calvino's exclusion of erotic detail in literature, as expressed in his 1961 article. Falaschi notes that the corrections
of the first edition of *Ultimo viene il corvo* to *I racconti*, denote,
among other things, the elimination of "le situazioni 'sconce' e
quei particolari piccanti che nel '58 Calvino dovette sentire come
una estremizzazione non necessaria o comunque compiaciuta di
situazioni osées" ("obscene" episodes and those racy details that
in 1958 Calvino must have felt were *osées* situations taken to an
unnecessary or at any rate indulgent extreme).[29] Here are a few
of the examples Falaschi reports among the many he finds:

1) From "Uomini e gerbidi," a "malizioso" reference to broth-
els, which includes this excerpt, is expunged: "Con donne, nude
sul petto e dietro; involte in stoffe di tutti i colori, che si ripetono
mille volte negli specchi" (With women, breast and backside

bared, wrapped in fabrics of all colors, who are repeated a thousand times in the mirrors).

2) From "Dollari e vecchie mondane," a segment which contains the image of a woman: "appoggiata di schiena all'uomo che le teneva le mani sopra i seni" (leaning back against a man who had his hands on her breasts).

3) From "L'avventura di un soldato": "[E questa piccola mano] s'accucciò tra coscia e coscia, buona e zitta in quel caldo e molle asilo, e" ([And this small hand] curled up between her thighs, quiet and well-behaved in that warm, soft shelter and).[30] This excerpt is also missing from the short story as it was included in the 1970 edition of *Gli amori difficili*; all the above excerpts are missing in subsequent reprintings of the 1949 edition.

For Falaschi, these, and other variants, reflect Calvino's abandonment of "la poetica neorealistica," but, in light of the article on eroticism, also indicate Calvino's putting into practice what he shortly thereafter preaches. Let us examine the trilogy *I nostri antenati*, written through the course of the fifties, for other examples of this reticence toward erotic detail and the search for a more forceful, less banal way of representing erotic impulses, emotional and physical (in Calvino they are usually indivisible).

In *Il visconte dimezzato*, the love of the two half-Medardos for Pamela is vital to thematic development as well as plot movement. From a thematic viewpoint, Pamela has, broadly speaking, been interpreted as a positive symbol of Nature, or of a communion with natural life, in contrast to Medardo's abnormal schism into a cruel half and an annoyingly beneficent half. Her life with the duck and the goat and her easy adaptation to forest life as a refuge from the sinister Medardo support this general interpretation, although Calvino's handling of this carefree yet shrewd female figure is far from serious, and sometimes tongue-in-cheek. As regards plot movement, Pamela is the romantic reason for the rivalry between the two halves and provides the impetus for the duel which ultimately serves to reunite them, and to rectify the abnormal and unnatural split. Thus, as symbol of Nature, Pamela is both impetus and goal, essential thematically as well as narratively.

Despite Pamela's romantic role, however, erotic undertones are almost absent in this novella-cum-fable. While a certain courtship, a certain exchange of romantic messages, is traced through the Medardos' courtship, very few references are made either in the narrative or in the dialogue to sexual impulse or to erotic desire. For example, the lepers' licentiousness is described thus by the child narrator:

> La porta s'aperse e ne uscì una donna olivastra, forse saracena, semi-nuda e tatuata, con addosso code di aquilone, che cominciò una danza licenziosa. Non capii bene cosa successe poi: uomini e donne si buttarono gli uni addosso agli altri e iniziarono quella che poi appresi doveva essere un'orgia.[31]

> The door opened and an olive-skinned woman, maybe Saracen, half-naked and tattooed, wearing kite's tails, came out and started a licen-tious dance. I couldn't clearly make out what happened next: men and women threw themselves on top of one another and began what I later learned must have been an orgy.

Such matter-of-fact observations are appropriate coming as they do from a child's perspective. The quip Pamela makes when retorting to the righteous Medardo's definition of love as doing "good" actions together has provocative undertones. "Peccato," she says, "Io credevo che ci fossero altri modi" (Too bad ... I thought there might be other ways), but Medardo ignores her comment (Calvino, *Il visconte dimezzato*, p. 75). The one com-ment that hints at erotic desire and the potency of the evil Me-dardo's quicksilver love for Pamela mocks the rationalization of Medardo's "decision" to fall in love with Pamela:

> Ma i pensieri che egli aveva freddamente formulato non devono trarci in inganno. Alla vista di Pamela, Medardo aveva sentito un indistinto movimento del sangue, qualcosa che da tempo più non provava, ed era corso a quei ragionamenti con una specie di fretta impaurita. (P. 53)

> But the thoughts he had coldly formulated must not deceive us. Upon seeing Pamela, Medardo had felt an indistinct stirring in his blood, something he had not felt in years, and he had hastened to that reasoning in a sort of fearful rush.

Both the mention of fear and arousal hint at the powerful kind of impetus love provides for the cruel Medardo, who always gets his way, except, mysteriously, with Pamela, whom he seems un-willing to coerce.

As in *Il visconte*, love is pivotal to the plot and themes of *Il cavaliere inesistente*. In a parody of the web-like intricacies and entanglements of unrequited love in epic poems, and with roots especially in Ariosto's *Orlando furioso*, greatly admired by Calvino, this novel, published eight years later in 1959, traces lovers' movements and mishaps. The plot follows Rambaldo's movements toward Bradamante, Bradamante's toward Agilulfo, Torrismondo's ultimate movement toward Sofronia, and Agilulfo's ensuing disappearance. As in the epic poems, one of the fundamental catalysts to plot is love, the desire to obtain one's love object. Love is also essential to the general themes of existence vs. nonexistence, or, put another way, identity, for the two young male warriors are searching for their identity, for adulthood. The quest for identity becomes entangled thematically with their desire; Calvino explains in the 1960 Introduction: "Per il giovane, la donna è quel che sicuramente c'è; e feci due donne" (For the young man, the woman is that which definitely exists; and so I made two women).[32] When Rambaldo goes crying in search of Bradamante, the narrator (Bradamante-Suor Teodora) observes, "a un certo punto l'innamoramento di lei è pure innamoramento di sé" (at some point, being in love with her is also being in love with himself—Calvino, *I nostri antenati*, p. 66). The intriguing relation between self and love will be explored further in later chapters; having sketched the pertinence of love in this text, let us move to some of the linguistic representations of eros.

There are three episodes which include female nudity, traditionally the home ground for erotic detail. One of these episodes, which deals with Agilulfo and Gurdulù's adventures in Priscilla's castle, nonetheless describes in detail none of the many indiscriminate sexual exploits of the squire, nor Priscilla's nudity. The language used to describe Bradamante's sexual union with Rambaldo parodies the stylized descriptions in early Italian literature. Their frantic coupling is summarized by the words, "si congiungono" (they are joined—p. 104), whose brevity and economy is reminiscent of *The Decameron*. While such a concise present-tense clause renders the eager rapidity of this much-awaited act of consummation, Calvino lingers not at all on descriptions of foreplay or the body. Yet one might expect more of an account, since the reader as well as Rambaldo and Bradamante (who believes she is finally sleeping with Agilulfo) have been waiting with anticipation for this sexual encounter.

Even richer for our purposes is the scene of Bradamante's urination, which is also the moment of love-at-first-sight for Rambaldo. The incongruity of this unlikely coincidence sets the absurd tone for the entire scene. Bradamante becomes Rambaldo's love object at the moment of urination! Schneider calls it "the quintessentially (and demystifyingly) female posture of urinating."[33] Her urination coincides with his falling in love with her; consequently, the stylized description of Bradamante's beauty coincides with the description in lofty and euphemistic terms of the act of urination. While the lofty language may be appropriate to render her beauty, it strikes us as ludicrous and jarring when employed for so "unromantic" an act as discharge.

The scene is organized in a sort of crescendo. At first her nudity is described: "un liscio ventre piumato d'oro, e tonde natiche di rosa, e tese lunghe gambe di fanciulla" (the smooth belly feathered in gold, and round rose-colored buttocks, and the taut, long legs of a girl—p. 38). Nothing unusual here. Her idealized form is rendered through stylized description, in the use of such traditional colors as "oro" and "rosa," common in descriptions of female figures through the ages. In addition, "ventre piumato" and "fanciulla" are semantic choices that befit this "chivalric" atmosphere. However, the lofty tone immediately buckles in the next sentence, in which the same sort of language combines with a colloquialism for urination. To take an excerpt from this sentence: "si mise tranquilla e altera a far pipì" (calm and lofty, she began to pee). The next sentence presents the paradigm of the linguistic and thematic collision Calvino has staged: "Era una donna di armoniose lune, di piuma tenera e di fiotto gentile" (She was a woman of harmonious moons, of a soft feather and a genteel stream). He is describing here, with the most proper, elevated language, her rear end, her pubic hair, and the flow of her urine, which he calls "genteel"! "Rambaldo ne fu tosto innamorato" (Rambaldo fell in love with her at once), the narrator concludes, in the ultimate parody of chivalric love (Calvino, I nostri antenati p. 38).

We are torn between laughing disbelief and fascination, as semiotic codes clash. The friction between urination on the one hand, and beauty and love, serious and oftentimes "sacred" literary themes, on the other, as well as the linguistic tension between the lofty, poetic language that describes her beauty and, euphemistically, her urination, explodes quite a few traditional codes—demystifies them, so to speak. First, we have a parody of youthful love-at-first-sight; secondly, an undercutting of the chivalric codes; thirdly, the language traditionally accepted for the description of female beauty is parodied. Finally, Calvino seems to be poking fun at our most romantic preconceptions. (Is this what he means by an eros restored to its rightful place as simply part of our nature?) Yet Bradamante undoubtedly begins to affect Rambaldo. Calvino has skillfully captured the erotic spark which will fuel Rambaldo's action, and fused it with the parody of that same eros.

A similar demystification occurs in Torrismondo and Sofronia's love scene; she is also described in idealized terms, and the description does carry a certain erotic impact, reminiscent of Boccaccio's Cimone coming upon the sleeping Ephigenia, who has a calming, civilizing effect on him (*Decameron*, bk. 5, 1). The description is rendered evocatively and fluidly by the polysyndetic structure:

> quelle lunghe nere ciglia abbassate sulla guancia piena e pallida, e la tenerezza di quel corpo abbandonato, e la mano posata sul colmo seno, e i molli capelli sciolti, e il labbro, l'anca, l'alluce, il respiro. (Calvino, *I nostri antenati*, p. 97)

> those long black lashes lowered over her full, pale cheek, and the softness of that relaxed body, and her hand resting on her full breast, and her soft, loose hair, and her lip, her big toe, her hip, her breath.

The erotic impact depends not only on the choice of physical detail, but also in the adjectives which imply fullness, softness and abandon: "piena," "tenerezza," "abbandonato," "colmo," "molli," and "sciolti." However, none of Calvino's heroines—and this seems to be almost unequivocal—are ever ingenues. Even Sofronia, a virgin, learning of Torrismondo's desire—in euphemistic terms, "il sentimento che mi ha infiammato" (the feeling which has inflamed me)—glibly and offhandedly tells him, "Oh, non fatevi scrupoli, sapete, ne ho viste tante. Benché, ogni volta, quando si arriva al punto, salta su il salvatore, sempre lui [Agilulfo]" (Oh, put your scruples aside. I've seen so much, you know. Though, each time, when you get right down to it, the rescuer leaps out, always him [Agilulfo]—p. 97). Once again, a certain erotic overtone is achieved, but underlying it are humor and the demystification of some of the codes of virginity and knighthood at the foundation of "chivalry." The actual act of consummation is in no way described and is intimated by an ellipsis.

In *Il barone rampante*, love episodes are less humorous, more serious. In his article, Calvino indicated that, given the impossibility of actually describing the sexual act in positive, innovative ways that would assign it the "natural" place it should have in the value system, poetic figures of speech offer a writer the most options. We have already seen various ways in which Calvino employs a poetic form of description, especially of the female form. In *Il barone*, the use of poetic imagery to render an erotic situation is even more prevalent and is, in fact, rarely undermined by humor or parody. However, as Calvino said in the preface to the 1960 edition of *I nostri antenati* and as Woodhouse and others have pointed out, Calvino took Cosimo more seriously than his other characters, and even identified with him.[34] As for the young knights, love is fundamental to Cosimo's development, as we will later see, but his experiences are handled delicately by the author. For example, in Cosimo's encounter with Ursula, who is his first lover, if not his first or greatest love, the image of the rose prevails, and in this poetic and erotic figure *par excellence* Calvino condenses the sensual evocativeness of the encounter. The metaphor of picking the "rosa rampicante" (climbing rose) creates the atmosphere of intimacy and a certain innocence, for picking the rose has often symbolized a deflowering, which in this case may be seen as a sort of mutual operation. In fact, Calvino uses the "rosa rampicante" and the "mandorlo tenero ma non vasto" (the tender but not large almond tree) to poetically underline the sensuality of the scene. These plants also circumstantially bring the two together, so the sensual imagery has a double function, and a double impact. It is a scene of adolescent purity almost, for there are no explicit sexual references, merely she as "ansante e rossa" (panting and red) and then the hugging and kissing. Calvino writes, "Così cominciò l'amore" (Thus love began), a love which is marvelously and surprisingly "semplice" (simple).[35]

A contradiction?

The two theses set forth in this chapter seem suspiciously at odds with each other.

The chapter began with the declaration of the importance and prevalence of the erotic factor in Calvino's texts, an element which has been sadly neglected, especially in comparison to the avalanche of studies on other aspects of Calvino's narrative. We recall, for example, Segre's statement that eros had rarely appeared in Calvino's texts prior to *Se una notte*. [36] Even Schneider feels that Calvino's use of eroticism is secondary in importance, and merely metaphoric.

However, our affirmation of the importance and the prevalence of the erotic element in Calvino's fiction was immediately followed by an article in which Calvino declared, in a tone so uncompromising, caustic and extremist as to be almost uncharacteristic of this cautious intellectual, that he frowned upon the use of erotic detail in literature. This as an editor, as well as a

writer. It is impossible, he claimed, for someone who is a friend
of sex in life to be one in literature. A brief look at the linguistic
choices of some of his romantic or sexual episodes before, or
during, the time he published the article (i.e., 1961), suggests
that he was reticent about the details of sex. To summarize our
points on this reticence: Falaschi's philological work with *I racconti* indicates that Calvino eliminated some of those "earthier"
details typical of the neorealist movement. This can be seen as
a rejection of the neorealist poetics, as Falaschi indicates. Calvino said in the 1960 preface to *I nostri antenati*, "era la musica
delle cose che era cambiata: la vita sbandata del periodo parti-
giano e del dopoguerra s'allontanava nel tempo" (it was the
music of things that had changed: the disbanded life of the Parti-
san and postwar period was receding in time.[37] But the elimination of "earthy" detail constituted a rejection too of that vision
of sexuality as "animalistic" in a negative sense, the perception
of sexuality as base, as sinful. *Gli amori difficili* sports very few
explicit details. In fact, even the long foreplay of the *soldato* is
fairly circumspect. In *Il visconte*, the erotic details are fewer and
given matter-of-factly. In *Il cavaliere*, the descriptions are stylized
and appropriate to the "chivalric" atmosphere, but also overlaid
with a satirical veneer, while in *Il barone* love is rendered in
beautiful, poetical language.

There appears to be a contradiction. How can we claim eros
as important, even fundamental, to Calvino's fiction and point
out at the same time how skimpy erotic detail is, and even posit
why it is so? And in this way explain why eros in Calvino has
failed to command critical attention? Several considerations
arise from this apparent contradiction. Does Calvino change his
view of erotic detail in literature after 1961? In the absence of
abundant erotic detail, how does Calvino portray the impact and
force that eros carries? His essay clearly implies that literature
is not up to a positive portrayal of sex, that it lies beyond the
threshold of literature's realm. In the following section, we will
examine in what way Calvino continues to believe what he wrote
in 1961 and in what way he mitigates his extremist view. We will
also explore Calvino's theories on literature's relationship to the
ineffable and his "battle" with language.

The theory transformed

The fundamental and most remarkable difference between the
1961 article and a later article from 1969 is that in the 1969

piece Calvino underscores the special place and unique role of the erotic in literature, and refers to his own use of the erotic in his writing. He also establishes the connection between the erotic in literature and in life—an eroticizing literature which should reestablish the importance of the erotic connection in life, broadly speaking.

However, in the 1969 article, a more complex and abstruse essay that requires close scrutiny, several points made in the earlier article resurface for greater exploration and development. For example, Calvino reasserts that an accurate rendering of sexual activity as a fact of everyday life is not possible:

> Ciò che occorre a questo punto stabilire è se in questo quadro può trovare posto l'intento smitizzante d'una rappresentazione diretta, oggettiva, spassionata, dei rapporti sessuali come fatti di vita in mezzo agli altri fatti della vita. Se questo atteggiamento fosse possibile esso occuperebbe non solo un luogo centrale, in opposizione tanto alle censure interne della repressione e dell'ipocrisia quanto alle speculazioni sacrali o demoniche sull'eros, ma sarebbe senz'altro la vincitrice, sgombrerebbe il campo di tutte le altre. L'esperienza letteraria degli ultimi cinquant'anni ci persuade però che questa posizione resta una pretesa intellettuale e illuministica.[38]

> What it is necessary at this point to establish is if within this framework the demythicizing intent of a direct, objective, dispassionate representation of sexual relations as facts of life among other facts of life can find a place. If this attitude were possible, it would not only occupy a central place, in contradiction as much to the many internal censorings of repression and hypocrisy as to the holy and demonic speculations on eros, it would without a doubt triumph. It would sweep the field clean. The literary experiences of the last fifty years, however, persuade us that this position remains an intellectual, rationalistic claim.

Calvino continues to view the portrayal of the erotic in literature as an oscillation between "apologetica" and "vituperio," the one an "esaltazione trionfalistica" (triumphalist exaltation) and the other a "discesa agli inferi della 'miseria della carne'" (descent into the nether world of the "misery of the flesh"—p. 213). However, Calvino no longer attributes these extreme positions almost entirely to society's inability to place the erotic aspect in its proper and natural position on the scale of values. We recall that Calvino, in 1961, condemned the hindrances that society's conflict with sex poses for an adequate representation. Neither obsession, whether in the form of condemnation or exaltation, does it justice; both rather impede its representation in literature and art. In the later article, Calvino wonders instead why the pessimistic handling predominates and why the "apologetica" treatment, the positive representation, having reached a high level of "mistificazione retorica," is impossible except at the level of massmedia. He attributes this to the progressive "desessualizzazione" (desexualization) of our times, promoted by the fight for survival in the cities. This is offset by the creation of a "sexual mythology" in the mass media, a mythology which has the function of compensating for a dimension "che si sente già perduto o fortemente in pericolo" (that is experienced as already lost or strongly endangered—Calvino, "Il sesso e il riso," p. 214). Although, unfortunately, Calvino does not expound on his definition of "desessualizzazione," one can only presume that he is referring to the fast-paced and impersonal existence that characterizes city life and contributes to the further alienation of individuals from their senses. The resulting mythicizing of sex in mass media seems to be causing a reactionary favoring of the negative handling in literature, according to Calvino.

Another reason for the difficulty of a "realistic" portrayal of the erotic, in the contemporary social context he describes, is that "il linguaggio della sessualità ha senso infatti soltanto se è posto al culmine d'una scala di valori semantici" (sexual language makes sense, in fact, only if it is placed at the top of a semantic scale of values—p. 213). Sexual language, in the broadest sense, comes into play when the "note più acute o delle più grave," or "i colori più accesi" (the sharpest or most solemn notes or the brightest colors) are necessary.

> Nell'universo del linguaggio, questa è la funzione del segno del sesso: esso non può uscire dalla sua posizione previlegiata, infrarossa o ultravioletta, ed è la connotazione positiva o negativa che accompagna i segni del sesso in ogni singola produzione letteraria a diventare determinante d'ogni sistema d'attribuzione di valori interno al testo. (P. 213)

> In the universe of language, this is the function of the sexual sign: it cannot step outside its privileged, infrared, ultraviolet position, and it is the positive or negative connotation that accompanies the sexual sign in each individual literary work that becomes the determining factor for every system for attributing values within the text.

Having said this on the literary function of sex and the present state of "literary" affairs, and addressed briefly the "desessualizzazione" of modern society, he goes on to sketch summarily some possible interpretations of the sexual aspect of the works of some authors such as D'Annunzio, D. H. Lawrence, Henry Miller, and Samuel Beckett.

We can draw two significant conclusions from such comments from the essay "Il sesso e il riso": 1) that sex is an exceedingly important literary motif, not to be ignored, and significant in understanding the essence of a work; and 2) that this literary effect derives from sex's function in life as an exceedingly important and potent everyday force that defies literary representation. One might say that there appears to be a split in Calvino's views between sex as a normal "fact of life" and its "ultraviolet light" function in literature. However, a glance at the affirmations that precede these conclusions will show this is not so, and we refer specifically to those ideas central to the article—the relationship between sex and laughter.

For Calvino, the link between sex and laughter is anthropological, and not merely "anticipo impaziente della felicità sperata" (impatient anticipation of the hoped-for happiness—p. 212).

> Perché il riso è pura difesa della trepidazione umana di fronte alla rivelazione del sesso, è esorcismo mimetico—attraverso lo sconvolgimento minore dell'ilarità—per padroneggiare lo sconvolgimento assoluto che il rapporto sessuale può scatenare. L'atteggiamento ilare che accompagna il parlare del sesso può essere dunque inteso non solo come anticipo impaziente della felicità sperata, ma pure come riconoscimento del limite che si sta per varcare, dell'entrata in uno spazio diverso, paradossale, "sacro." (P. 212)

> Because laughter is a pure defense mechanism of human fear in the face of sexual revelation. It is mimetic exorcism—through the minor upset of hilarity—for mastering the total upset that sexual relations can trigger. The attitude of hilarity that accompanies talk of sex can thus be understood not only as an impatient anticipation of the hoped-for happiness, but also as a recognition of the boundary that is about to be crossed, of the entrance into a space that is different, paradoxical, "sacred."

Calvino probably puts "sacro" in quotations here to distinguish it from the strictly religious connotation, and to designate it a mysterious and sensitive area. Sex is recognized as a powerful and unsettling force, as one that thus provokes trepidation. Eros is here defined by Calvino as a "sacred" territory and "per molti l'approccio di segni del sesso si è svolto tradizionalmente attraverso il codice del gioco, del comico, o almeno dell'ironico" (for many, the approach to the sexual takes place traditionally through the codes of play, of the comic, or at least of the ironic— p. 211). Both the ideas of sacredness and humor in a discussion of the artistic representation of eros bring to mind several other articles which address and clarify Calvino's fundamental perception of his own creative procedure and the writer's—storyteller's, narrator's—relationship to words and language. These articles also illuminate Calvino's ideas on sexual representation and show how deeply rooted in Calvino's theory of artistic creation his theory on erotic language is. The articles we will briefly consult are Calvino's famous "Cibernetica e fantasmi" ("Cybernetics and Ghosts") on the technique of ars combinatoria, published in 1967, only a few years before his article on sex and laughter, and a critical essay by the renowned art historian E. H. Gombrich which Calvino quotes in this article. Gombrich's piece is entitled "Freud e la psicologia dell'arte" and was published in an eponymous volume in 1967 by Einaudi, the publishing house for which Calvino worked.

Those familiar with Calvino's theoretical work know that he rejects the Romantic notions of originality and genius as hallmarks of the great artist. In "Cybernetics and Ghosts," in a typically provocative fashion, Calvino posits the idea that computers may be equipped to take on the task of writing. He feels that language is a mechanism, a machine made up of elements that can be put together and taken apart not in infinite combinations, but in finite combinations that are nonetheless multitudinous. The first tribal narrator had a limited amount of words with which he could play and "test the extent to which words could fit with one another, could give birth to one another."[39] The modern writer faces the same limits, even if his choice of words has increased considerably. In his vision of language as ars combinatoria, Calvino includes the theories of linguists who have broken language down into "codes and messages" (Calvino, "Cybernetics and Ghosts," p. 10), of structuralists like Greimas who "analyzes the narrative quality of all discourse, which may be reduced to a ratio between what they call actants," of the neo formalist school that "employ[s] . . . the results of cybernetic research and structural semiology" (p. 11), and finally of the experimenters in France in the OULIPO, to which he would later belong, that explore the relationship between mathematics and language. All of these modern schools advance the concept of literature not as an outpouring of the unconscious, as the expressionists and surrealists thought, or as an expression of genius in the Romantic sense, but as reducible to a mechanism. Calvino says that the author, "that spoiled child of ignorance," should disappear "to give place to a more thoughtful person, a person who will know that the author is a machine, and will know how this machine works" (p. 16).

If any should think that Calvino here is being tongue-in-cheek, or at least *entirely* tongue-in-cheek, let us refer to his explanation, in this same article, of his own writing process:

> Literature as I knew it was a constant series of attempts to make one word stay put after another by following certain definite rules; or, more often, rules that were neither definite nor definable, but that might be extracted from a series of examples, or rules made up for the occasion. (P. 15)

He goes on to affirm:

> What Romantic terminology called genius or talent or inspiration or intuition is nothing other than finding the right road, following one's nose, taking shortcuts, whereas the machine would follow a systematic and conscientious route while being extremely rapid and multiple at the same time. (P. 15)

He very firmly believes that literature's potential is completely contained in the language, which echoes Gombrich's observations in his article ("I giochi di parole non vengono fabbricati: sono scoperti nel linguaggio" [Word games are not invented: they are discovered within language]).[40] It also echoes Paul Klee's comments on visual art cited by Gombrich: "Sono essi [linea, colore, forma] a decidere 'se un certo contenuto possa rimanere inesprimibile nonostante la più favorevole disposizione psicologica'" (It is they [line, color, form] that decide "if a certain content must remain inexpressible despite the most favorable psychological disposition").[41]

However, something *does* save the artistic process from falling into the hands of computers. In his *Six Memos*, Calvino offers Leonardo da Vinci's struggles as "l'esempio più significativo d'una battaglia con la lingua per catturare qualcosa che ancora sfugge all'espressione" ('the most significant example of a battle with language to capture something that still evades expression').[42] This battle with language is also addressed in the "Cybernetics" article. Calvino, in the second part of this article, takes the opposite view, because he says—characteristically playing both sides—that taking the opposite view is the best safeguard against becoming "trapped in the spiral of one's own thoughts" (p. 18). He then discusses literature's struggle to say what has not been said, and asserts that this is its goal, its aspiration; literature must trespass into the realm of the inexpressible and unutterable. The following impassioned and eloquent passage redeems literature from its status as product of a mechanical process:

> But is the tension in literature not continually striving to escape from this finite number? Does it not continually attempt to say something it cannot say, something that it does not know, and that no one could ever know? A thing cannot be known when the words and concepts used to say it and think it have not been used in that position, not yet arranged in that order, with that meaning. The struggle of literature [more literally translated: *the battle of language*] is in fact a struggle to escape from the confines of language; it stretches out from the utmost limits of what can be said; what stirs literature is the call and attraction of what is not in the dictionary. (P. 18, italics mine)

A quick glance back at the article on sex and laughter identifies the erotic as one of the domains in which language fails, because the erotic too is "indicibile": it defies all attempts to render it precise and falls into "a mysterious obscurity" (p. 211).

> In letteratura la sessualità è un linguaggio in cui quello che non si dice è più importante di quello che si dice . . . Perfino agli scrittori la cui immaginazione erotica vuole oltrepassare ogni barriera, accade d'usare un linguaggio che, partendo dalla massima chiarezza, passa a una misteriosa oscurità proprio nei momenti di maggiore tensione, come se il suo punto d'arrivo non potesse essere altro che l'indicibile. (P. 211)

> In literature, sexuality is a language in which that which is not said is more important than that which is said . . . It happens that even writers whose erotic imagination would like to surpass every barrier use a language that, starting from the utmost clarity, passes into a mysterious obscurity precisely at the moment of greatest tension, almost as if the point of arrival could be nothing but the inexpressible.

Calvino calls this attempt to describe the erotic a "movimento a spirale per aggirare e sfiorare l'indicibile" (a spiral movement to circle and skim the inexpressible—p. 211). The erotic dimension

is "sacred" territory that both challenges and eludes representational methods. How? In "Cybernetics," Calvino, in his assessment of "the battle of language," asks, "But what is a language
vacuum if not a vestige of taboo, of a ban on mentioning something, on pronouncing certain names, of a prohibition either
present or ancient?" (p. 19). These prohibited territories, he later
tells us, constitute the realm of the unconscious, and therefore
deal with primal human truths too powerful to face (presumably,
death, sex, incest, etc.). "The unconscious is the ocean of the
unsayable, of what has been expelled from the land of language
. . . until literature redeems these territories and annexes them
to the language of the waking world" (p. 19). It is as if the erotic
might be in a state of exile and, by extension, literature must
seek to "redeem" it.

Thus we can better understand Calvino's impatient intolerance, in both the 1961 and 1969 articles, of the obsession with
sex as "sin" or "myth," and especially of the diluted, tired form
it takes in the mass media. These observations, clearly, underscore how the erotic for Calvino is one of those "unspeakable"
truths, those dreams, those inhibitions, that are too powerful or
frightening for the individual or society to face. For these reasons, sex has an "ultraviolet" function in art for Calvino and its
"place" in daily life defies representation. As part of the unconscious, it eludes definition, detail. Calvino's view of the erotic
poses some tough artistic dilemmas. On the one hand, it remains
unexplained and inexplicable, an unsettling human experience
fraught with intensity. On the other hand, literature must constantly seek to try to say something about that which is unsayable, that which has remained unsayable because no words have
yet been found.

Calvino, Gombrich—and Freud

Not surprisingly, perhaps, a perusal of Calvino's love stories
discloses fairly scanty evidence of treatment of eros as the very
serious, threatening, "sacred" force that he deems it here. Our
several brief analyses have shown as much. In fact, as some have
noted, and as any reader of Calvino will also note, humor seems
to characterize Calvino's handling of love situations. We think of
Bradamante and the moment Rambaldo falls in love with her.
We remember all the light and amusing love episodes in *Le cosmicomiche* which from its very title invites the reader into a

comic world. S. di Bucci Felicetti goes so far as to say, "In tutti i casi comunque l'esperienza erotica sarà in Calvino coniugata con il segno comico" (In all cases, however, the erotic experience will, for Calvino, be united to the comic).[43] While this assessment in its generality undercuts the complexity and versatility of love in Calvino's fiction (We recall, for example, the blending of death and love motifs in *Sotto il sole giaguaro* and in *Il castello*), Calvino does often give love relationships a comic twist.

Humor, as a device linked to the game motif, provides in fact the backdrop for a resolution of tensions between the concept of writing as mechanism, the necessity of saying the unsayable, and sex's relation to laughter. The resolution between these three elements can be found in Gombrich's article on Freud published at the same time as "Cybernetics and Ghosts." Calvino quotes Gombrich in his article on cybernetics, which appeared just two years before the article on sex and laughter. Perhaps Gombrich's article was even instrumental in the development of Calvino's erotic theories. However, it must also be mentioned here that very rarely is Calvino's name linked to that of Freud. Having claimed his own lack of interest in "psychology" and acknowledged by critics as "rationalist" rather than as deeply sentimental, Calvino has often been considered—rightly or not—as a proponent of order rather than as an adventurer into the unconscious.[44] However, through Gombrich, Calvino upholds some of Freud's theories on art.

Gombrich notes that for Freud the child's pleasure in word games, in games with language, is a pleasure connected with the acquisition of the mastery of language. He then points out that there exists a certain affinity between poets and one who plays word games.[45] As Calvino puts it, referring to Gombrich's article, the pleasure originates from a certain fortuitous combination, a certain juxtaposition of words that suddenly causes

> things [to] click into place, and one of the combinations obtained— through the combinatorial mechanism itself, independently of any search for meaning or effect on any other level—becomes charged with an unexpected meaning or an unforeseen effect which the conscious mind would not have arrived at deliberately: an unconscious meaning, in fact, or at least the premonition of an unconscious meaning.[46]

Gombrich, in fact, reminds us that Freud said "il motto di spirito" (the joke) could be explained by this formula: "'Un'idea

preconscia è esposta per un momento all'influenza dell'incon-
scio'" (A preconscious idea is exposed for a moment to the influence of the unconscious) and that

> il concetto di arte resiste al fatto di essere esteso oltre il punto in
> cui il rapporto quantitativo tra il materiale inconscio e l'elaborazione
> preconscia non è mantenuta entro certi limiti.[47]

> the concept of art resists being stretched beyond the point where the
> quantitative relationship between unconscious material and precon-
> scious elaboration is not kept within certain limits.

To say it another way: playing with the materials of one's art—
literature or another—can result in a successful combination of
artistic tools, a juxtaposition that becomes charged with an "unexpected meaning" that suddenly accesses a deeper plane of
meaning. This discovery redeems from the world of the "unsayable," of the unconscious, something that "is of great concern to
the author or his society."[48] So, while a literary machine can
produce combinations, it cannot create "meaningful" combinations, impact, or shocking effect. The poet or writer, on the other
hand, can recognize the particular effect a fortuitous word game
can have on the individual or on society, for the artist is
equipped—unlike machines—with both a conscious and an unconscious. Thus the concept of play is pivotal to Calvino's perception of the writing process, as well as to literature's attempt to
explode societal taboos. Calvino's *ars combinatoria* is ultimately
liberating rather than mechanistic, because it brings to light, to
consciousness, hidden truths.

The pleasure principle which, according to Calvino and Gombrich, unites the child's word games with that of the poet, implies that laughter can be liberating in so far as it is a method of
handling/controlling upsetting thoughts that expose subcon-
scious desires and associations that disturb us. It is within this
context that we can understand Calvino's legitimization of laughter as a way of facing the erotic. Calvino reminds us not to forget
the deep tie, on an anthropological level, between sex and laughter. Given these considerations, his comment (quoted above and
repeated here) on the connection between sex and laughter acquires new meaning:

> Perché il riso è pura difesa della trepidazione umana di fronte alla
> rivelazione del sesso, è esorcismo mimetico—attraverso lo sconvolgi-
> mento minore dell'ilarità—per padroneggiare lo sconvolgimento as-

soluto che il rapporto sessuale può scatenare. L'atteggiamento ilare che accompagna il parlare del sesso può essere dunque inteso non solo come anticipo impaziente della felicità sperata, ma pure come riconoscimento del limite che si sta per varcare, dell'entrata in uno spazio diverso, paradossale, "sacro." (Calvino, "Il sesso e il riso," p. 212)

Because laughter is a pure defense mechanism of human fear in the face of sexual revelation. It is mimetic exorcism—through the minor upset of hilarity—for mastering the total upset that sexual relations can trigger. The attitude of hilarity that accompanies talk of sex can thus be understood not only as an impatient anticipation of the hoped-for happiness, but also as a recognition of the boundary that is about to be crossed, of the entrance into a space that is different, paradoxical, "sacred."

Summary

In conclusion, a writer trying to effectively render the erotic has a number of obstacles to contend with, according to Calvino: the narrow morals and obsessions of a distorted societal view of sex; the mythicizing of sex in a desexualized society and the difficulty of avoiding tired, pretty clichés in trying to write positively about eros; the human reaction to this primitive and frightening impulse; and the struggle to represent this sacred, unspeakable domain of human experience—a representation which Calvino feels must necessarily be indirect. Calvino feels that literature must do battle with all these impediments; and laughter, for him, offers one way of dealing with the erotic force, of bringing it in a new and shocking way into wakefulness, out of the unconscious. Calvino also sees laughter as "modestia della parola di fronte a ciò che è troppo al di là della parola, di contro alla rozza pretesa che un linguaggio sublime o serioso potrebbe avere di darne 'l'equivalente'" (the modesty of the word in the face of that which goes too far beyond the word, in contrast to the coarse pretension of a sublime or grave language to give its "equivalent").[49]

While in the 1961 article Calvino discouraged the representation of sex in literature, in the 1969 article, Calvino recognized that an increasingly desexualized urban world challenges literature to reestablish a healthy and strong connection between life and eros as life force. Extreme measures are necessary to redevelop an erotic relationship between the individual in the world and the world. We might say that such extreme measures and such goals could form Calvino's "moral option" in the realm of the erotic. It is in this light that we can understand the prevalence of cosmic love—perceived as the connection between human and life force at all stages of evolution—in his fiction. At the end of his 1969 article, among the "esperienze letterarie che si svolgono sotto il segno del riso" (literary experiences which take place under the sign of laughter), Calvino numbers Beckett's experiments and his own experiments in Le cosmicomiche, which we will explore in the next chapter. He concludes the complex article "Il sesso e il riso" thus:

> Come volevo dimostrare, solo il riso—irrisione sistematica, falsetto autoderisorio, smorfia convulsa—garantisce che il discorso è all'altezza della terribilità del vivere e segna una mutazione rivoluzionaria. (P. 214)

> As I wished to demonstrate, only laughter—a systematic derision, a self-mocking falsetto, a convulsive grimace—guarantees that the discussion is equal to the tremendousness of life and signals a revolutionary change.

3

"Il Movimento a Spirale":
Sex, Language and Laughter

As we have seen in the preceding chapter, the ramifications of Calvino's untitled essay on the erotic in *Nuovi argomenti* and "Il sesso e il riso" in *Una pietra sopra* are numerous. In the first of these, Calvino adamantly states that one must not add to the ongoing representation of the sexual in literature and intimates that partly due to society's obsession with sex and partly due to the elusive nature of the erotic, it is best not to write about sex at all. Yet in the second article, while he seems to be reiterating in an attenuated tone his earlier convictions, i.e., that sex is difficult to represent positively and directly in literature and art, he is at the same time affirming the opposite of what he said earlier. His second article, understood in light of the article "Cybernetics and Ghosts" and Gombrich's article on Freud, tells us that sex is "sacred" territory, shrouded in silence, steeped in taboos, and that it is the obligation of the writer to illuminate such mysteries, to break the taboos, to bring difficult truths back into the realm of consciousness. In essence, his later position seems to be vastly different from the one articulated in the 1961 essay.

Clearly, the next step would be to examine Calvino's fiction in light of the notions he has articulated, to study the combination of sex and laughter, and the perception of eros as a cosmic force. At the end of the second article, Calvino says that he tried in literature to do what the "arti plastiche" are trying to do for visual art, namely to "stabilire una comunicazione erotica con i materiali e gli oggetti della nostra più squallida vita quotidiana" (establish an erotic communication with the materials and objects of our most squalid everyday life). He tried to do this by "immaginando rapporti sessuali non antropomorfi" and "raccontando amori di molluschi o di organismi unicellulari" (imagining nonanthropomorphic sexual relationships and recounting the loves of mollusks or unicellular organisms—Calvino, "Il sesso e il riso," p. 214). He is obviously alluding to *Le cosmico-miche*. While his allusion can be interpreted as a metonym for the entire collection of Qfwfq stories, which deal with sundry nonanthropomorphic sexual relations, read more carefully, the specific allusion is to *two* stories: "La spirale," in which Qfwfq is a mollusk, and "Priscilla," in which he is a cell. (The latter was published originally in *Ti con zero*.) These short stories, which explore almost exclusively the themes of erotic desire and its expression, have many similarities. Critics such as De Lauretis, Friedman and Bernardini Napoletano have also seen the connection between these two stories. De Lauretis sees "Mitosi" as "parallel" to "La spirale"[1] while Friedman sees "Priscilla" in its entirety as an "elaboration of 'La spirale.'"[2] The stories also offer an exemplification of some of the ideas discussed above.

The image of the spiral, around which the eponymous story is thematically organized, reappears in the second story as well and may function as an illustration or symbol of Calvino's ideas of the erotic and its representation in literature. In "Priscilla," he uses the term when he is discussing his composition as a nucleus; the image of the spiral refers to the components of the nucleus. He in fact quotes Borek's *Code of Life* in the series of (for the most part) scientific epigraphs that introduce this and all the tales of *Le cosmicomiche*. Calvino quotes Borek's use of the image of the spiral in the explanation of duplication of DNA.

> Se i due filamenti si separano come le due metà d'una chiusura lampo e ogni spirale serve di modello perché si formi una spirale complementare, ecco garantita la duplicazione esatta del DNA e quindi del gene.[3]

> If the two filaments separate like the two halves of a zipper and every spiral serves as a model in order to form a complementary spiral, this guarantees the exact duplication of the DNA.

In the narrative itself, Calvino fuses the scientific image of the spiral with his own earlier story ("Priscilla," as part of *Ti con zero*, was published after *Le cosmicomiche*), so that his use of the image in "Priscilla" resounds with the self-referential allusions as well as with a scientific one. The following is a passage excerpted from one of the page-long sentences characteristic of the style in the story:

e tutto quello che io ero e tutto quello che io andavo via via essendo finiva per risultare nel nucleo ed esservi assorbito registrato accumulato in un serpentino attorcigliarsi di *spirali*. (Calvino, *Cosmicomiche*, p. 253, italics mine)

and all that I was and all that I, by and by, was becoming ended up in the nucleus and was absorbed, recorded, accumulated there in a serpentine coiling of *spirals*.

Interestingly enough, this same image occurs in the essay on sex and laughter, and is used by Calvino to describe the inevitable way in which writers must approach and express the "indicibile." It becomes the symbol for a circumlocutory approach to the erotic in the arts.

Perfino agli scrittori la cui immaginazione erotica vuole oltrepassare ogni barriera, accade d'usare un linguaggio che, partendo dalla massima chiarezza, passa a una misteriosa oscurità proprio nei momenti di maggiore tensione, come se il suo punto d'arrivo non potesse essere altro che l'indicibile. Questo movimento a *spirale* per aggirare e sfiorare l'indicibile accomuna gli scrittori dell'erotismo più estremo, da Sade a Bataille, agli scrittori dalle cui pagine il sesso sembra rigorosamente bandito, come Henry James.[4] [Italics mine]

It happens that even writers whose erotic imagination would like to surpass every barrier use a language that, starting from the utmost clarity, passes into a mysterious obscurity precisely at the moment of greatest tension, almost as if the point of arrival could be nothing but the inexpressible. This *spiral* movement to circle and skim the inexpressible unites writers of the most extreme eroticism, from Sade to Bataille, to the writers from whose pages sex seems rigorously banned, like Henry James.

The image of the spiral thus functions in three different ways in these texts: in "La spirale," it is a literal shell which is the product of an expression of desire; in "Priscilla," it represents the reproductive lowest common denominator; in the article, it symbolizes the circular, circumlocutory linguistic technique for portraying the erotic. However, all three texts in some way reflect Calvino's attitude toward sexual expression in the arts, and since Calvino refers to these stories at the end of the essay, as we have seen, these three interrelated pieces seem to constitute three points in an ongoing discourse. The recurring image of the spiral and the network it forms among the texts demands closer analysis.

Both Qfwfq tales explore the development of the individual identity. Interest in or desire for the Other plays an important role in this development, as well as in the subsequent relationship with the Other (referred to as "lei," the other mollusk, in "La spirale" and "Priscilla" in the eponymous story). Qfwfq the mollusk in "La spirale" exists in a state of blessed formlessness, feeling in himself "tutte le forme possibili" (all possible forms) and having no "limiti ai miei pensieri" (limits to my thoughts— p. 226). There are no images to think with, and no brain, but he thinks "semplicemente in quel modo indeterminato di sentirsi lì che non escludeva nessun modo di sentirsi lì in un altro modo" (simply in that indeterminate way of feeling oneself there that did not exclude any ways of feeling oneself there in another way—p. 226). He feels young, in a condition "ricca e libera e soddisfatta," "polpa di mollusco piatta e umida e beata," (rich and free and satisfied . . . a flat and humid and lucky pulp of mollusk) but confesses to being something of a "narcisista" totally absorbed in himself, by himself, with himself (p. 226). Qfwfq, in "Priscilla," starts his study in the same way—by explaining that his state of being "innamorato da morire" (wildly in love), contrary to the readers' usage, had nothing initially to do with being in love with something else, but consisted initially of a sense of completeness and fullness derived from his existence as a cell. "Una cosa così basta e avanza a riempirti la vita" (Something like this is more than enough to fill your life), he says, and later in the same lengthy, discursive sentence: "io parlo d'un senso di pienezza . . . spirituale . . . cioè il fatto della coscienza che quella cellula lì ero io, era questa coscienza la pienezza" (I'm talking about a sense of spiritual fullness . . . that is, the fact of an awareness that that cell there was me, this awareness was the fullness—p. 249). The next stage for Qfwfq in both stories is the statement of an awareness of Otherness, that is, the awareness that there is a world out there, something other than the individual. However, at this point, the stories diverge a bit, with a slight shift in focus. For example, Qfwfq the mollusk immediately notes other masculine and feminine entities and one feminine mollusk in particular he has been responding to. In his "anthropomorphized" feelings of insecurity and jealousy so common to love, in his inability to gauge her reactions or even his own impact on her, he decides to DO something, something which would serve to mark his presence and his individuality, his distinctness. This thing is the spiral, and it is interesting to note that this object which, impelled by erotic feeling, he creates, later becomes, as he says, "una difesa per la mia sopravvivenza che guai se non me la fossi fatta" (a defense for my survival—how awful for me had I not built one—p. 230). The erotic thrust in essence is essential to Qfwfq's developing identity, as well as an expression of his identity: "Così io facevo la conchiglia, cioè solo per esprimermi" (So I made the shell, that is, only to express myself—p. 230).

Unlike Qfwfq the mollusk, Qfwfq the cell does not immediately identify the Other as the feminine, but rather attempts to define the impetus toward the Other and all its ramifications, which we will analyze more in depth a little further on. Yet Qfwfq the cell says that desire spurs him also to "fare, a fare qualcosa, ossia a fare qualsiasi cosa" (to do, to do something, or rather to do anything—p. 255) which echoes "La spirale": "lo sforzo di fare qualche cosa, ossia qualsiasi cosa, ossia tutte le cose" (the effort to do something, or rather anything, or rather everything—p. 231). For Qfwfq the cell this "doing" becomes "saying": "e siccome l'unica cosa che avevo da dire era me stesso, ero spinto a dire me stesso, cioè a esprimermi" (and since the only thing that I had that I could say was myself, I was impelled to say myself, that is, to express myself—p. 255). For both the cell and the mollusk, the erotic impulse results in a form a self-expression as a way of doing, as a form of action.[5] At this point, however, the focus of the stories more definitively diverges, as Qfwfq the mollusk seeks to find the individual feminine he loves among all feminine creatures while the cell embarks upon an attempt to explain the attraction between himself and Priscilla. However, there is another echo of the earlier story in the very last section of "Priscilla," the section which is entitled "Death": "sopra di noi si estende un altro tetto, il guscio di parole che noi continuamente secerniamo" (Another roof stretches above us, the shell of words which we continually secrete—p. 271). This seems to refer directly to the earlier story, for the "guscio" reminds us of the shell and "secernere" is the verb used to describe the act of making the spiral: "Fu allora che mi misi a secernere materiale calcareo" (It was then that I began to secrete calcareous material—p. 229).

Although the two stories do diverge, we can see that there are many similiarities—thematic, narrative, and metaphoric. In both, the awareness of the self, manifested in a sort of self-love, is necessary for the love story. The expression of desire is another step toward the fuller realization of self because expression of desire, whether sexual, evolutionary or artistic, is a form of growth. Another similarity is that both stories focus on the state preceding desire and its fulfillment, i.e., the beginning stages of love. We know that Calvino tends to favor beginnings. In fact, in most of his fiction, this initial stage, the beginning of the love story, is the part which dominates. Many of the stories in *Gli amori difficili* focus on this initial moment, as do many of *Le cosmicomiche* and two of the three stories in *Sotto il sole giaguaro*.

In the "Mitosis" section of "Priscilla," Calvino, through Qfwfq, attempts to give an explanation why it is often the beginnings of the love story that are recounted, told, elaborated. In the first four paragraphs of "Priscilla," Qfwfq talks about his sense of plenitude as a cell as he embarks on the telling of a past love story—of which, however, he remembers very little. These four paragraphs also contain some of the fundamental motifs as well as the philosophical and scientific context of the rest of the relatively long (for Calvino) short story. In fact, if parts of the story are less developed than others—Qfwfq explains—it is not because they were less important. They are, he says, merely

> meno sostenute dalla mia memoria, in quanto ciò che mi ricordo bene è la fase diciamo iniziale della mia storia d'amore, quasi direi la fase precedente, cioè sul più bello della storia d'amore la memoria si disfa si sfilaccia si tagliuzza e non c'è modo di ricordarsi cosa succede dopo. (Calvino, *Cosmicomiche*, p. 250)

> less sustained by my memory, in so far as that which I remember well is the—let's say—initial phase of my love story, almost—I would say—the preceding phase, that is, at the best part of the love story memory comes undone, it unravels, it goes to shreds, and there's no way to remember what happens later.

Previously, Qfwfq had confessed that even the little he remembered was enough to "sconvolgermi dalla testa ai piedi" (to unsettle from head to toe) and repeats this expression later in the same lengthy sentence. This description brings to mind the article on sex and laughter in which Calvino referred to sex as "sconvolgimento": "lo sconvolgimento assoluto che il rapporto sessuale può scatenare" (the total upset that sexual relations can trigger—p. 212). It seems that memory functions selectively to protect the individual from such upset. Calvino intimates that this very protection from upset expresses itself in a focus on beginnings; thus the phases "preceding" love become characteristic of the love affair as Calvino defines it: "Non ricordarmela è a un certo punto necessario perché la storia sia questa e non un'altra, cioè mentre di solito una storia consiste nel ricordo che se ne ha, qui il non ricordare la storia diventa la storia stessa" (Not remembering it is at a certain point necessary so that the story is this one and not another, that is, while in general a story consists of the memory one has of it, here not remembering becomes the story itself—p. 250). This very ambiguous statement suggests other parallels between "Priscilla" and the articles on sexual representation: the author seems to confirm that the essence of the love story lies in its resistance to representation, whether in visual images or in language, even within the memory, because of the amount of upset—or better, "sconvolgimento"—involved. Once again, love seems to be situated in the realm of the unconscious and the "sacred," while it remains the struggle of language to try in some way to render these experiences, to recover them from those forbidding, heavy, dark veils. We recall Calvino's insistence on, and lifelong commitment to, precision in language, and will later see that Qfwfq the cell consciously struggles for "precision" in expressing his love story.

However, there are several other considerations to be made before embarking on a study of the "metafora del linguaggio" in "Priscilla" (p. 256). First, the emphasis that Qfwfq places on the consciousness of self as the beginning of his state of "innamoramento" immediately spills into an assertion of the near impossibility of an "objective" account of a love story, albeit a past one. Acknowledging that the little he remembers of the love story is "sconvolgente," Qfwfq affirms,

> se dicevo oggettivamente dicevo così per dire, come si dice quando si dice oggettivamente che poi dài e dài finisci sempre per dare nel soggettivo, e così questo discorso che voglio farvi mi è difficile proprio perché dà tutto nel soggettivo. (P. 250)

> If I said "objectively," I said it in a manner of speaking, like when one says "objectively" and then you end up in the subjective, and so this talk I wanted to give you is really difficult for me because it gives way completely to the subjective.

Partly because emotions are involved, partly because a point of view is always subjective, Qfwfq is pronouncing the absolute subjectivity of his discourse, affirming the personal aspect of the discussion because it is bound by the limits of the individual (even an individual as extraordinary and omnipresent as the protean Qfwfq).[6] At the same time, Qfwfq is affirming the "relativity" of his discourse, thereby refuting any pretension to an absolute discourse. In the fourth paragraph, in fact, theories of relativity play a part in his discussion of time sequences. This initial phase of the love story he will relate is initial because it is what he remembers as the first, not the first in an absolute sense. Thus he has defined his terms and the limits of his discussion: the I, its subjectivity, the powerful and overwhelming impact of eros, its resistance to representation, and the relativity of time sequences.

In these same four paragraphs, there is also a linguistic feature characteristic of much of Calvino's writing and even more of *Le cosmicomiche*. The adverb "cioè" (that is) appears six times just in these beginning paragraphs, and "o meglio" another variation, appears once as well. Other variants, such as "ossia," "oppure," "vale a dire," and "anzi," for example, are numerous throughout the Qfwfq stories and riddle both "La spirale" and "Priscilla" perhaps even more than the other stories. In "La spirale," in fact, "cioè," "ossia" and "vale a dire" occur twenty times, although the first two are far more prevalent than the latter. V. Mengaldo has also identified these characteristics in much of Calvino's work and recognized their prevalence, and their significance, in *Le cosmicomiche*. His observations are worthy of attention:

> Alla radice di molti fatti dello stile di Calvino ho posto l'esigenza, quasi la coazione a distinguere e graduare. Ma l'espressione più paradigmatica per frequenza, articolazione, significato, ne è il complesso di fenomeni che possiamo comprendere, dilatandola, sotto la classica categoria della *correctio*. Distinguendo velocemente le modalità, ecco le *correctiones* vere e proprie, in funzione di una migliore messa a fuoco (formule come *anzi, o meglio, o almeno* . . .); le indicazioni di compresenza, che costeggiano o invadono quel gusto dell'ossimoro che risponde in profondo alla logica e visione della realtà sempre a due facce propria di Calvino (*e insieme, e nello stesso tempo* . . .); le indicazoni di alternativa (*ossia, oppure, sia . . . sia* ecc); *correctiones* attenuanti o precisanti formulate in termini metalinguistici (*dico, oserei dire* . . .).[7]

At the roots of many aspects of Calvino's style I have placed the necessity, almost the compulsion to distinguish and grade. But the form of expression that is most paradigmatic in frequency, articulation and meaning is that sum of phenomena that we can include, by stretching it, under the classical category of the *correctio*. Quickly distinguishing the modalities, we have the real *correctiones*, which function to better focus (formulas like *rather, or better, or at least* . . .); indications of dual presence, that border or pervade that predilection for the oxymoron that corresponds at heart to the logic and vision of an always two-sided reality typical of Calvino (*and also, and at the same time* . . .); the expressions of alternatives (*or, or rather, both . . . and,* etc.); attenuating or specifying *correctiones* formulated in metalinguistic terms (*I say, I would dare to say* . . .).

After cataloguing other examples of "formulazioni correttive e probabilistiche" (corrective and probabilistic formulations) as symptomatic of Calvino's "coazione a distinguere e graduare," Mengaldo observes: "una vera e propria sovrassaturazione, e insieme una tematizazzione, del fenomeno esplodono nelle *Cosmicomiche*" (a real oversaturation, as well as a thematization, of the phenomenon explode in *Cosmicomiche*).[8]

Such a phenomenon may be particularly prevalent and suited to the subject matter of Calvino's experimental text for many reasons. For example, the alternatives that such expressions introduce reflect the rich potential of a world in its primitive stages, captured in almost every story at that precise stage before the earth changes or evolves into something else, maybe not better, but different, or maybe better, but not without loss of something that previously existed and that cannot coexist alongside the new. The stylistic phenomenon Mengaldo notices might function as a reflection on a linguistic, stylistic, and semantic level, a sort of linguistic parallel to the world of infinite possibilities, the magical state of latency that many critics have recognized as the context of these stories, and which the stories themselves underscore. In "L'origine degli uccelli," Qfwfq captures a moment in which "tutto ritornava possibile" (everything became possible again—p. 39), and "La spirale" comes to mind as another example, for Qfwfq the mollusk also feels in himself "tutte le forme possibili" (p. 226). Thus these linguistic markings are particularly suited to render the potentiality of the world in evolution.

However, because the subject matter for many of these stories is the world before the creation of language, the world before human beings, such "corrective" language is particularly appropriate, in that it attempts to render, in human language, experiences that occurred before it existed. Thus, Calvino's need to "distinguere e graduare" acquires a new significance here. We find a good example of this in "La spirale" also: "Forma non ne avevo, cioè non sapevo d'averne, ossia non sapevo che si potesse averne una" (I did not have a form, that is, I didn't know I had one, or rather I didn't know it was possible to have one—p. 225).

Calvino, who upheld and advocated a "precise language" both for himself and other writers, as well as for politicians and everyone else, uses these linguistic devices to render more precisely prelanguage phenomena.

However, ironically enough, in "La spirale," and even more so in "Priscilla," the use of these correctives does not bring the reader any nearer to an understanding of the phenomenon being described. Sometimes, the correctives in fact further confuse the issue. The descriptions are too complex to be grasped by human logic, and are almost poetic in their elusiveness. For example, Qfwfq the mollusk, imagining the (female) mollusk with whom he is in love, says, "Ossia, non che mi immaginassi le forme che lei avrebbe potuto prendere, però mi immaginavo la particolare qualità che lei, prendendole, avrebbe dato a quelle forme" (Or rather, it wasn't that I imagined the forms she might have taken, but I imagined the particular quality that she, taking them, would have given to those forms—p. 228). The "precisions" more than anything else resemble poetry, which a certain key might make more comprehensible. Ironically, for all its scientific pretensions to precision, such a revised statement only hints—like a poem— at a possible meaning.

The "Priscilla" story contains even greater pretensions toward a precise telling of a love story and confounds the reader even more (although it differs from the "mathematical and deductive exercises," as some critics have called them, of *Ti con zero*). So we must ask ourselves, is Calvino playing with us—again? Is he indicating that precision is impossible, or even inadvisable and undesirable? That seems paradoxical, unlikely even, in the face of his heated reiterations on precision. A precise language is surely one of the components of that mysterious but essential "morale" that he claims (just before his death in Corti's interview with him) has linked his more than four decades as writer. Perhaps another statement on language as precision will help clarify his position, and put an end to any (though tempting) notions of a writer who is weaving linguistic labyrinths around his readers, a writer wilfully shielding himself from being "understood."

In a 1984 interview granted to G. Lucente, Calvino addresses "the combination of clarity and complexity" of his style:

> What I'm interested in doing is to seek out—if it's the case to clarify, at any rate to represent—complexity. What is complex interests me, what is knotted up and difficult to describe, and I try to depict it in a style as limpid as possible.[9]

Thus Calvino tries to represent *complexity*, and we know that he certainly considers the erotic to be a complex phenomenon. He states, however, that he does not try to create a "mimesis of complexity through language that is like a boiling cauldron, through a representation that is complex in itself and that calls attention to itself," as do Gadda or Edoardo Sanguineti.[10] Nor is he like Joyce or Faulkner. He states, "My procedure is different because I try to deepen the contrast between sentences that are apparently linear, classical, and a reality that is undeniably complex."[11]

The operative word here is "apparently." Calvino appears to be presenting a "linear" sentence, a straightforward representation, and using correctives for clarification, especially in the two stories we are discussing. However, because of the indeterminacy of the prelinguistic context, the complexity of individual identity and its relation to the Other, the sentences in fact underline the imperviousness, the inscrutability, the very intricacy—and thus the rich "irreducible" phenomenon—of human existence in all its dimensions.

Calvino, in "Priscilla," presents this very dichotomy between precision and complexity, between the explicable and the "indicibile."[12] Calvino, in his attempt to explain love in its most basic form, chooses the most basic life form, the cell. He selects the lowest common denominator as protagonist, the smallest building block, in order to facilitate the explanation of a complex phenomenon. However, as we have seen, Qfwfq defines his terms by relinquishing immediately any claims to objective, absolute truth and by describing the love for the Other in the most preliminary, pre-Other terms, before he embarks on a description of his love for the feminine Other.

In his description of his love for what is outside him, Qfwfq states that the "emptiness" he feels is "the world and the future" in the cosmic sense, all that is not him: "tutto il possibile."[13] "Ed ecco che traboccavo d'amore per questo altrove altravolta altrimenti muto e vuoto" (And here I was overflowing with love for all that elsewhere other time otherwise—Calvino, *Cosmicomiche*, p. 252). Having explained that he is not "innamorato da morire" of himself but of everything that is outside himself, he goes on to describe himself and his interior life—his nucleus— as a cell. Like Qfwfq the mollusk, he is "giovane, sano, nel colmo delle mie forze" (young, healthy, at [his] peak—p. 253). He is determined in his nucleus by a series of spirals, or filaments, or twigs or little sticks, or chromosomes, and says, "ognuno di

questi . . . aveva una precisa relazione con qualche particolarità
di quello che io ero" (and each of these . . . had a precise relation
to some of the particularities of what I was—p. 253). He says
that he might even go so far as to affirm that he is nothing but
the sum of those filaments, reducible to a number of filaments,
merely a sum of the parts. In the same way, we could deduce,
anticipating what is to come, that literature is nothing but the
ars combinatoria achievable by the computer Calvino mentions
in his article, "Cibernetica e fantasmi." However, Qfwfq states
that "c'è qualcosa che non è rappresentabile con quei bastoncini,
un vuoto . . . Cioè quella tensione verso il fuori l'altrove l'altrimenti, che è poi quel che si dice uno stato di desiderio" (there
is something that cannot be represented by those little sticks, a
void . . . That is, that tension toward the outside the elsewhere
the otherwise, which is what is termed a state of desire—p. 254).

This elaborate metaphor about the internal life of the cell hints
at that part of the individual identity which cannot be reduced
to, explained by, the analysis of its parts. It indicates the existence
of an irreducible human component—desire, the erotic drive. Its
portrayal as cosmic and cellular slowly changes, as we will see,
into a portrayal of three representations of Priscilla.

Although Qfwfq has said that this desire is not representable
by the "little sticks," he attempts through language to further
specify what he means. Here is the first in a series of (doomed?)
thrusts to be more "precise":

> Su questo stato di desiderio è meglio essere più *precisi*: si verifica
> uno stato di desiderio quando da uno stato di soddisfazione si passa
> a uno stato di crescente soddisfazione e quindi, subito dopo, a uno
> stato di insoddisfacente soddisfazione cioè di desiderio. (P. 254, ital-
> ics mine)

> On this state of desire, it would be better to be more *precise*: a state
> of desire occurs when from a state of satisfaction one passes into a
> state of increasing satisfaction and then, immediately afterwards,
> into a state of dissatisfying satisfaction, that is, desire. (Italics mine)

Although this statement offers some illumination, it is clearly
not "precise." Nonetheless, Qfwfq continues to explain how simple desire turns into a desire for Otherness. The next paragraph
begins in a similar way, with another indication of what becomes
in this first section a motif: "Per precisare questo punto m'ac-
corgo che sono tornato a parlare in termini generali, perdendo il
terreno guadagnato con le precisazioni anteriori, cosa che spesso

succede nelle storie d'amore" (In order to make this point more precisely, I realize that I have gone back to speaking in general terms, losing the ground I gained with the earlier precise statements, something which often happens in love stories—p. 255). Qfwfq is attempting to define something which in some way defies analysis—the love story.

Qfwfq goes on to explain that his desire becomes a desire to *do*, which in the absence of an external world means for him *to say*: "ero spinto a dire me stesso, cioè a esprimermi" (I was driven to say myself, that is, to express myself—p. 255). "Sarò più preciso," he says again, and introduces overtly that which had been implicit: the metaphor of language. Qfwfq's language is "tutti quei bruscolini o stecchini detti cromosomi" (all those little sticks or toothpicks called chromosomes—p. 255). Qfwfq's growth and changes as a cell are his own language, his very identity is also his self-"expression," just as the spiral of Qfwfq the mollusk is both his creation and his identity. The self becomes the message.

A digression which might serve as another illustration of this equation of self as message, of expression as identity, might perhaps be in order to underscore the coherence and the repetition of this theme that seems fundamental to one of Calvino's visions of love. In "L'avventura di un automobilista," the story which ends the 1970 edition of "avventure" (and which was not part of the 1958 series of "avventure" in *Racconti*), written at about the same time as "Priscilla," shows another very blatant representation of self as the very message in love. This story has undergone various analyses as a prime example of structural composition and *ars combinatoria*.[14] The narrator who is driving in the rain to his lover's house after a fight realizes that he hopes that she too is driving toward him and that his rival is driving toward her as well, as if the rival were essential to validating the chase. Thus the message that the narrator hopes to receive is "questo cono di luce" (this cone of light)[15] and so is the message he hopes to transmit, because these would be pure messages of desire, uncomplicated by "la complessità delle nostre persone e situazioni ed espressioni facciali" (the complexity of our persons and circumstances and facial expressions—Calvino, *Gli amori difficili*, p. 106). "Priscilla" renders some of the complexities of expressing and defining personality that the narrator may be hinting at here. The narrator of the "avventura" wishes that they may "ridurre noi stessi a comunicazione essenziale" (reduce [themselves] to pure communication—p. 106). The difficulty in communication is the complication of personality, etc. A clear, unequivocal, unmistakable message *could* be expressed, however, if they were "liberati finalmente dallo spessore ingombrante delle nostre persone e voci e stati d'animo, ridotti a segnali luminosi, solo modo d'essere appropriato a chi vuole identificarsi a ciò che dice . . ." (finally freed from the cumbersome thickness of [their] persons and voices and moods, reduced to signals of light, the only way to be for whoever wants to identify himself with what he says—p. 108). We are reminded of the metaphor of language in "Priscilla," of saying the self, of the doing that is saying. This desire to become a message, here a cone of light, recalls "La spirale" and the mollusk's doing which is also saying. It recalls all the struggles between lovers to communicate, to transmit messages and the anxiety that the message—the message of the individual who is the message—might not be received.

To return to *Le cosmicomiche*: both the mollusk and the cell are moved to growth and self-expression by *desire*, certainly in a cosmic sense, but undoubtedly also in an erotic—and heterosexual—sense, for the Other is always female. Language ironically becomes a metaphor for this growth and expression. "Quindi bastava ripetere quei bruscolini o stecchini per ripetere me stesso, si capisce per ripetere me stesso in quanto linguaggio" (So it was sufficient to repeat those little sticks or toothpicks in order to repeat myself, clearly, to repeat myself as language), Qfwfq says, extending the metaphor, and referring to multiplication of the self and by extension to the procreative act as well.

However, he stops, saying that if he continues to "fare *precisazioni* all'interno di altre *precisazioni* non ne esco più. E' vero che qui bisogna procedere con molta attenzione per non cadere in inesattezze" (continue to make *precise statements* within other *precise statements* [he] won't be able to make [his] way out of them. It is true that here it is necessary to proceed with great caution so as not to fall into inaccuracies— Calvino, *Cosmicomiche*, p. 255, italics mine). Once again, he makes explicit reference to the necessity for precision, yet a certain dramatic irony prevails, because the network of metaphors becomes increasingly difficult to unravel. Cellular reproduction is a metaphor for the state of being in love; language is a metaphor for this reproduction and the medium for its representation as well.

It might be well to mention at this point that in Qfwfq's explanation of the halving of chromosomes of which mitosis—and cellular reproduction—consists, there surfaces a series of images evocative of male arousal and sexual activity, as evidenced in the description, "m'era preso un bisogno di stirarmi quant'ero largo, fino a una specie *d'irrigidimento* spasmodico dei nervi che non avevo" (I was struck by a need to stretch myself out to my full width, to a sort of spasmodic *stiffening* of the nerves I didn't have) and the mention of an explosion, evocative of male climax, in the "scoppio del nucleo" (explosion of the nucleus—p. 256, italics mine). Perhaps it is these evocative images in "Priscilla" that G. Fink is referring to when he says,

> sono le pagine più oscure e alessandrine del libro, e al tempo stesso le più inequivocabilmente erotiche di uno scrittore che, nonostante le parolacce d'obbligo del *Sentiero dei nidi di ragno*, resta ancora assai alieno dalle parentesi 'amorose' (significativa la totale improbabilità di Claudia, la *covergirl* della *Nuvola di smog*.)[16]

> They are the darkest and most Alexandrine pages in the book, and at the same time the most unmistakably erotic for an author who, despite the requisite dirty words in *Sentiero dei nidi di ragno*, still remains quite averse to "amorous" parentheses (to this effect, the total improbability of Claudia, the *cover girl* of *Nuvola di smog*).

Fink, like other critics we have mentioned, seems to feel eroticism in Calvino is a rare occurence. Interestingly enough, this critic finds Claudia more of an improbability than the eroticism of the cellular entities here described.

As Qfwfq the cell continues to describe the feelings and process of chromosomal halving, which in this first story becomes the preparatory stage for future love, the attempts at precision continue. "Bisogna qui precisare" (It is necessary here to be more precise—Calvino, *Cosmicomiche*, p. 257), he says. Then, in that attempt to correct, to be more precise, he adds,

> prima ho usato il verbo ripetere, che come al solito era un po' approssimativo . . . e anche il verbo dire era piuttosto fuori luogo . . . in quanto per dire ci vuole uno che dica e qualcosa che sia detto, e questo allora proprio non è il caso.
> Difficile insomma definire in termini precisi l'indeterminatezza degli stati d'animo amorosi. (Pp. 257–58)

> first I used the verb "to repeat," which as usual was a little approximative . . . and even the word "to say" was rather out of place . . . since in order to say you need a someone who says and a something that is said, and this then is absolutely not the case.

Difficult, in short, to define in precise terms the indeterminacy of amorous frames of mind.

No metaphor is perfect, and thus language as a metaphor for chromosomal halving is as approximate as it is in its role as medium of representation of the state of being in love. At this point, Qfwfq is reminding us that he is the thing he is telling, that his own growth is his own telling, and that all of this is the erotic impulse toward that emptiness, that outside, that elsewhere, that is not—yet—him. Love, in fact, seems a waiting for this outside, this Otherness, and consists of feelings that are typically associated with a state of desire: impatience, joy, greediness, jealousy and pain. These emotions are to some extent present in many of Calvino's lovestruck protagonists.[17] In his split at the nuclear level, Qfwfq realizes that "il mio uscire da me stesso è un'uscita senza ritorno" ([his] coming out of [him]self is a departure without a return—p. 259).

The motif of the inability to return to a previous stage, or state, and the resulting sense of irrecoverable loss recurs throughout Le cosmicomiche.[18] Certainly, in the evolutionary process, with every step gained something is lost. In "Priscilla," it is the plenitude of self, the unity of self that is lost through a desire for Otherness and a world under transformation. But in that moment before "il dopo" which is plurality, before the loss of "completeness" of self which is the future, defined as "cellule asimmetriche che sommano i messaggi ripetuti attraverso trilioni di trilioni d'innamoramenti mortali" (asymmetric cells that sum up the messages repeated across trillions and trillions of human falling-in-loves—p. 259), Qfwfq is able to see the future and reconcile plurality and unity in the way Qfwfq did in "L'origine degli uccelli," to see the continuity, the discontinuity of the continuous, as Calvino might say.[19] He repeats that he understood. He recognizes the existence of "un se stesso pluricellulare e unico" and "un se stesso unicellulare e innumerevolmente plurimo" (a multicellular unique self [and] a monocellular countlessly multiple self—p. 260). He concludes, at the end of "Mitosis," recalling again the story of the birds, that it is the union of past and present, that one feels at the moment of separation, that is essential. In that moment of union which is the separation of the self from the self, in that moment of "sconvolgimento," of upheaval, of upset, Qfwfq (in "L'origine degli uccelli") is on the verge of understanding the continuity of past and future, the similarities between two worlds. Significantly, the "act of love" defined as a union which requires a loss of self, offers the possibility of such vision. Consequently, in that moment of "strappo da me stesso" (the rending from myself) of the cell, Qfwfq already anticipates his love for Priscilla, who takes the startling form, at the end of the first section, of an elegant, sexy English woman living in Paris.

Throughout *Le cosmicomiche*, including "La spirale" and "Priscilla," Qfwfq is often both human and not human; Qfwfq is a living creature, very rarely a man, who is nonetheless entirely anthropomorphized. Qfwfq, in his many love affairs, pursues the feminine in the shape of Dutch girls, an elegant Englishwoman, queen bees, etc. in both the present and the prehistoric past. Through Qfwfq, Calvino can give love a cosmic breadth, and redeem the erotic as a powerful evolutionary force, as a powerful emotion, as the impetus toward expression, as the force behind *all* forms of creation, and the act of creation itself. He redeems it from the dark and tired visions he condemned in his articles. At the same time, his analogies between human, cellular, and mollusk love are immediately comic, from a linguistic as well as a narrative perspective, and this humor—as we know from the 1969 article—serves to attenuate the seriousness of the discussions at hand.

The humor becomes even more pronounced in "Meiosi" as Qfwfq attempts to explain the relationship between himself and Priscilla and decides that it is first necessary to define his terms, as he did in the preceding section. Unfortunately, the story he purports to tell is never told because those very tools—the schools of modern thought—which are used today to define the makeup of the individual, are here exposed by Calvino as detrimental to the uniqueness of the individual—the individuality of the individual, so to speak. Thus, a love story is impossible because it becomes impossible to define "io" and "Priscilla." In an ironic parody of scientific and psychological theories which would define the two terms—"io" and "Priscilla"—these very rulers of human identify serve to undermine that very identity and to dehumanize and oversimplify the two subjects. We will see that the biological and psychoanalytic theories with which Calvino plays in this section are presented as parallels, complementary approaches that lead to the same discouragingly deterministic conclusions, although these theories have traditionally been viewed as in fierce opposition to each other.

Along similar—though more liberating—lines, the physical and emotional components of the erotic, i.e., the sexual drive and the emotional need, are reunited within the biological model. Qfwfq does this simply by pointing out that mental and physical relationships both involve millions of neurons gathering stimuli. This observation serves perhaps to reduce the "mythicizing" of the erotic Calvino objected to in his essays on sexual representation by bringing it back to its biological roots. It is noteworthy that, at the same time, the biological model frees the physical, i.e., the sexual—and often societally censored— dimension of the erotic from accusations of shame and ignominy.

So, before Qfwfq can depict a relationship, he must define the two who will have the relationship. This, he points out, is even more complicated than telling the story of only one cell. Before recounting their story, he must take into account the constant changing of the two subjects, himself and Priscilla. Once again, the very attempt at precision, the taking into account of all factors—temporal, spatial, biological, emotional—serves to further complicate. However, Qfwfq asserts that there is a basic, unchanging "programma stabilito" (fixed program—p. 261) in the two subjects which can be addressed. Particularly worthy of note is his next comment:

> Il problema insomma non è quello, ma forse sollevarlo non è stato inutile perché serve a farci capire che le cose non sono semplici come sembra e così ci si avvicina lentamenta al punto in cui capiremo quanto sono complicate. (Pp. 261–62)

> In short, that is not the problem, but maybe raising the issue has not been fruitless because it serves to help us understand that things are not as simple as they seem and so we slowly reach the point at which we understand how complicated they really are.

Clearly, Calvino is executing and at the same time drawing attention to his "movimento a spirale" ("Il sesso e il riso"). His propensity for linguistic correctives and semantic alternatives in language here acquires another meaning, namely that the circumlocutory approach is appropriate to the representation of complex issues.

Qfwfq then embarks on an explanation, in the broadest terms, of the relationship between his and Priscilla's "genetic patrimony" and their environment, which together determine their existences so completely as to deprive them of the possibility of a future; the future would be merely a result of, and therefore would be contained in, this cross between environmental and parental inheritance. Gradually evoking the notion of psychological determinism are his references to the influence of the environment (p. 262, "E dicendo forma . . . fin da piccolo") and genetic predisposition: "su quarantasei cromosomi ventitrè mi vengono da mio padre e ventitrè da mia madre, cioè continuo a portarmi dietro i genitori in tutte le mie cellule, e non potrò mai liberarmi da questo fardello" (out of forty-six chromosomes, twenty-three come from my father and twenty-three from my mother, that is, I continue to drag my parents along with me in all of my cells, and I will never be able to free myself from this burden—p. 264). There is a sort of determinism in the Freudian sense through the continuing effect of one's parents; inside every cell "continuano a fronteggiarsi gli ordini contraddittori del padre e della madre" (a mother and father's contradictory orders continue to face off—p. 265). All these elements—environment, genes, upbringing—conspire to eliminate the future, and orchestrate instead "un programma stabilito con materiali che ci fabbrichiamo sempre uguali" (a fixed program with materials which we always make the same—p. 264).

It might not be amiss here to point out the parallels between these theories' attempts to lay bare the mechanisms—emotional, biological, physical—comprising human behavior and to reduce human beings to mechanisms, and Calvino's acknowledgment in the beginning of "Cibernetica e fantasmi" that writing is a mechanism that can be executed by computers as easily as by humans. One might say that humans, like writing, become the products of an—however sophisticated—ars combinatoria.

It is thus impossible, within the deterministic models Calvino alludes to, for anything to happen, because all has been forecast, all has happened,—"nothing is new under the sun." Qfwfq tells us, consequently, "fuori di me non ho né avrò rapporti con niente e con nessuno" (outside of myself I do not have nor will I have a relationship with anyone or anything—p. 263). In typically provocative Calvinian fashion, the "separation" from the self in "Mitosis" has in "Meiosis" been deemed—at least, momentarily—impossible. Calvino has been undermining the very methods of analysis he is employing; he has been satirizing science's attempts to measure human identity, individuality, and love, and shows that these phenomena are exceedingly difficult to "reduce" to an analysis. Qfwfq cautions at one point, "i termini della questione più li si semplifica più tornano a complicarsi" (the more you simplify the terms of the issue the more complicated they become—p. 263). Science, methodologies and mechanistic models have many limitations. As Hazard Adams has put it so well in his discussion of the relation that some writers and critics developed between science and art: "they clearly drew an analogy between art and scientific method; the weakness of the analogy was that scientific method reduces the unique and the individual to the species or to general law."[20]

The love depicted in "Meiosis" shares certain attributes with the love depicted in Calvino's other love stories (some of which are addressed in *Gli amori difficili*), and many critics consider these attributes characteristic of the erotic in Calvino. This passage reveals such crucial motifs as absence, impossibility of union, solitude and thwarted love:

> Priscilla, addio, l'incontro, l'abbraccio sono inutili, noi restiamo lontani, o già vicini una volta per tutte, cioè inavvicinabili.
> La separazione, l'impossibilità d'incontrarsi è già in noi da principio. Siamo nati non da una fusione ma da una giustapposizione di corpi diversi. (Calvino, *Cosmicomiche*, p. 264)

> Priscilla, good-bye, the meeting, the embrace are useless, we remain far apart, or close once and for all, that is, unapproachable to the other.
> The separation, the impossibility of meeting is within us from the beginning. We were born not from a fusion but from a juxtaposition of different bodies.

The union, in the literal sense, of two bodies who occupy the same space, who merge, and are thus metamorphosed into a third new being, is deemed impossible. Qfwfq describes the sex act in biological terms as a lack of union at the most basic biological level: sperm and egg do not fuse or mix. Further developing his metaphor of language, Qfwfq says that the "words" in both nuclei fit in their entirety. Once again, a biological truth underlines a sexual and emotional condition. The biological reality corresponds to the physical and affective meeting of two lovers who join but do not fuse. This is the "distanza incolmabile che separa in ogni coppia i due compagni, il fallimento, il vuoto che rimane alla coppia più riuscita" (the unbreachable distance that in every couple separates the two partners, the failure, the void that remains with the most successful couple—p. 265). This is the result not merely of the complete impossibility of action by Qfwfq and Priscilla, but also of the absolute "solitude" of the individual.

"Vuoto separazione e attesa, questo siamo" (Void separation and waiting, that is what we are—p. 266). The brevity of these poetic declarations of desperation underscores their importance in an otherwise complex spiral of descriptions, of sentences as long as paragraphs. They are themes common to poems through all time and strike us as particularly resonant compared to the "scientific" discussion on the reproduction of cells. Calvino has invested a singularly unpoetic and unerotic activity such as cell division with all the force of the human erotic drive.

The realization of the impossibility of individuality translates into the impossibility of a love relationship. Calvino has made it clear again and again that individual identity is a prerequisite for any amorous entanglement. The possibility of a love story between two individuals with a unique attraction for each other is precluded by all the determinisms. Qfwfq moans, "E noi abbiamo un bel correre, Priscilla, per venirci incontro e inseguirci . . . Noi non eravamo che la preparazione, l'involucro, all'incontro dei passati" (And we have quite a way to go, Priscilla, in order to meet and to pursue each other . . . We were nothing but the preparation, the wrapping, for the meeting of pasts—p. 267).

But, as we know, every issue has at least one other side for Calvino: the great advantage of this lack of newness is that it draws the lovers into a history of great cosmic love, an eros responsible for evolution. Calvino has widened his exploration of "cellular" love to embrace the entire cosmos. Eros is affirmed as a cosmic force that includes the smallest entity and all of Nature. The lovers participate in a cosmic force:

Così l'antica marea s'alza a intervalli in me e in Priscilla seguendo il corso della Luna; così le specie sessuate rispondono al vecchio condizionamento che prescrive età e stagioni degli amori. (P. 267)

So the ancient tide rises at intervals in me and in Priscilla following the course of the Moon; so the sexual species respond to the old conditioning that establishes the ages and seasons of love relations.

So, although he feels that the two of them are merely meeting places for such messages from the past, there is in the end of this second section a very positive, "happy"—if unexpected—ending. "La storia che volevo raccontare è l'incontro di due individui che non ci sono" (The story I wanted to tell is the meeting of two individuals who don't exist), Qfwfq concludes, only to correct himself one more time and to identify an "intervallo di vuoto che è la nostra presenza individuale" (interval of void which is our individual presence). This part comes into contact with "l'onda che continua a rinnovare . . . e questo basta a darci la certezza che qualcuno è 'io' e qualcuno è 'Priscilla' nella distribuzione spaziale e temporale delle cellule viventi" (the wave that continues to renew . . . and this is enough to give us the certainty that someone is "I" and someone is "Priscilla" in the spatial and temporal distribution of living cells—p. 268). This "vuoto" is that which defies measurement, that element which is not merely the result of nurture and nature, but is something else, that part which—according to Calvino—thwarts, evades and challenges artistic representation.

The very last sentence of "Meiosis" offers an image so vivid and colorful after the preceding logical spiralings that it startles the reader:

> Già questo [the certainty that the "vuoto" assures that an "I" and a "Priscilla" do exist] basta, Priscilla, a rallegrarmi, quando allungo il mio collo ricurvo sul tuo e ti do un leggero morso sul pelo giallo e tu apri le narici, scopri i denti, e t'inginocchi sulla sabbia. (P. 268)

> This [the certainty that the "vuoto" assures that an "I" and a "Priscilla" do exist] is enough, Priscilla, to cheer me, when I stretch my bent neck over yours and give you a light nip on your yellow hair and you flare your nostrils, reveal your teeth, and kneel in the sand.

The rhythm of this sentence is faster, more fluid, than the preceding ones, due to the polysyndeton and the abundance of l's and r's which give it poetic impact. At first, Qfwfq and Priscilla appear human, two lovers about to make love on the sand, but with the addition of the "gobba" (the hump) we realize that they are instead camels! The sentence continues:

> o che dolcezza quei tramonti nell'oasi ti ricordi quando ci slegano il carico dal basto e la carovana si disperde e noi cammelli ci sentiamo tutt'a un tratto leggeri e tu spicchi la corsa ed io trottando ti raggiungo nel palmeto. (P. 268)

> oh what sweetness those sunsets in the oasis do you remember when they unfasten the load from our pack saddles and the caravan scatters and we camels feel light all of a sudden and you break into a run and I at a trot join you in the palm grove.

The horizons of possibility, which seemed to have been slowly narrowing and closing in this section on determinism, suddenly open to a vision of desert and oasis. The moment of freedom from the pack saddles corresponds to the moment of freedom from the burden of determinism. "Non potrò mai liberarmi di questo fardello," Qfwfq had said earlier (p. 264), referring to his genetic patrimony.

The last part of the last section, "Morte," deals with mechanisms and machines directly. All our relationships, all our buildings, all our creations, are considered by Qfwfq to be a sort of language, in the broadest sense of the word. They are first self-expression, "il guscio di parole che continuiamo a secernere" (the shell of words which we continually secrete) and then "un sistema di comunicazione" (p. 271). The mechanisms that we are and the mechanisms that we create are overwhelming, suffocating. The equations that Calvino sets forth in this last section no longer seem to rise out of a positive vision of the cosmic force, of erotic love. The vision becomes apocalyptic:

Il soffitto che ci copre è tutto ingranaggi di ferro che sporgono: è come il ventre d'una macchina sotto la quale sono strisciato per riparare un guasto, ma non posso uscirne perché, mentre io sto schiena a terra là sotto, la macchina si dilata, s'estende a coprire tutto il mondo. (P. 272)

The ceiling that covers us is all iron gears that stick out: it is like the belly of a car I have slipped under, to repair some breakdown, but I cannot slide out because, while I am down there on my back, the car expands, stretches to cover the whole world.

This last section on machines, and specifically on electronic word-producing machines, recalls once again "Cibernetica e fantasmi" and its view of computers' role in literature. However, it is only the individual defined at the end of "Meiosis" as "intervallo vuoto"—a "vuoto" that no "bastoncini" can fill—that can give meaning to society. The individual, though not omnipotent, is central to Calvino's vision of the cosmos, as Hume has pointed out.[21] And that is how "Priscilla" ends, with the "io" and the "Priscilla" as two distinctive words meeting again . . . as humans, as camels, as machines . . . The erotic connection prevails.

Mengaldo's comments provide a fitting recapitulation of the points discussed in this chapter:

Ciò che in prima analisi appare culto della precisazione analitica e della sfumatura, rimonta certamente a un rapporto fra il soggetto, e il suo linguaggio, e la realtà concepita sotto il segno, insieme deludente e salutare, dell'indeterminazione. Atteggiamento a sua volta polivalente se non ambiguo, perché muove in pari tempo dalla percezione dell'irriducibile complessità del mondo (e anche del suo caos), da cautela nell'interpretarlo e da una sorta di eudemonismo intellettuale che esalta il gioco in se stesso delle congetture, alternative, sfumature, contraddizioni. In ogni caso ne è sollecitato quello che abbiamo chiamato relativismo linguistico: la lingua non può dire tutto e subito, ma *forse* riesce a dire *qualcosa*, a patto di circuirla e quasi corteggiarla con assidua pazienza, disposti allo scacco.[22]

What in the initial analysis appears to be a cult of analytical precision and nuances, certainly winds back to a relationship between the subject and its language, and reality as conceived under the sign, both disappointing and beneficial, of indeterminacy. An attitude polyvalent if not ambiguous in its turn, because it proceeds at the same time from a perception of the irreducible complexity of the world (and even of its chaos), from caution in interpreting it, and from a sort of intellectual eudaemonism that exalts the game in and of itself of conjecture, alternatives, nuances and contradictions. In any case, what we have called linguistic relativism is urged: language cannot say everything and quickly, but *maybe* it might succeed in saying *something*, by circling around it and courting it with assiduous patience, prepared for failure.

4

Another Interpretation of *Gli amori difficili*

In Calvino's famous 1960 preface to the trilogy, which is "a trilogy of experiences on how to realize one's potential as a human being" (Calvino, *I nostri antenati*, p. xix) and which plunges the reader into the problem of identity, Calvino describes the protagonist of *Il cavaliere inesistente*: "Rambaldo, paladino stendhaliano, cerca le prove d'esserci, come tutti i giovani fanno. *La verifica dell'essere è nel fare*" (Rambaldo, Stendhalian paladin, looks for proof of his existence, as do all the young. *The proof of being is in doing*—p. xvii, italics mine). Rambaldo's condition recalls that of Qfwfq the mollusk and the cell; both are young, and both need to *do* as a means of expressing themselves, of distinguishing their individuality.

Love, Calvino continues, is closely linked to this struggle for identity. "Per il giovane, la donna è quel che sicuramente c'è" (For the young man, the woman is that which definitely exists—p. xvii). Calvino then proceeds to explain that the internal struggles and needs of the two young male protagonists determine which female protagonist they will love.

Later, in the novel, when Bradamante is about to chase after Agilulfo, with whom she is madly in love, Rambaldo chases after her, unable to believe that she does not want him. He thinks, unaware of his self-centeredness, "sono qui, giovane, carico d'amore, come può il mio amore non piacerle?" (Here I am, young, full of love, how can my love not appeal to her?—p. 66). The narrator (Calvino, Suor-Teodora/Bradamante?) comments, "e a un certo punto l'innamoramento di lei è pure innamoramento di sé, di sé innamorato di lei, è innamoramento di quel che potrebbero essere loro due insieme, e non sono" (And at a certain point, his falling in love with her is also a falling in love with himself, with himself in love with her, it is falling in love with what the two of them could be together, and are not—p. 66). Rambaldo too seems subject to narcissism—a word which we find used, but modified, in "La spirale," and which is evoked but rejected at the beginning of "Priscilla." This narcissism is the basis of the desire for the Other; that is, this form of self-love in Calvino does not signify the desire to be adored or worshipped. This love of self provides a sort of cornerstone for the love of the Other.

From this perspective we can attempt a new exploration of some of the stories of *Gli amori difficili*. Although several analyses of this puzzling text (of lifeless vignettes, of neorealist "fette di vita"?)[1] have appeared in the past decade, it seems that these short stories remain—like the topos of love itself—largely neglected and misunderstood. Ricci feels all of the stories in *I racconti* have been neglected: "Little attention has been paid the *Racconti* as a measuring stick of the author's poetic temperament."[2] Friedman, at the end of her chapter on *Gli amori difficili*, notes, "*Gli amori difficili* are [sic] most often overlooked, not credited much importance in the body of Calvino's more startling and radical works"; she finds the collection to be important within the context of Calvino's *opus* because in it she sees the "seeds of much of what can be considered radical."[3]

Before the expanded 1970 edition came out, these short stories were published as part of the larger collection *I racconti* (except for "L'avventura di un soldato" and "L'avventura di un bandito" which appeared in *Ultimo viene il corvo*, the latter under the title of "Un letto di passaggio"). One might say they have been read in a negative key.[4] "Negative" synthesizes several critical perspectives. The narrative has been regarded a "failure" on the part of the author, as well as a narrative of "failure" and alienation successfully *executed* by the author.[5] Examples of these two readings appear in the introduction to the 1970 edition, attributed to Calvino, which includes criticism of *I racconti*.

One of the negative evaluations of the author's workmanship mentioned in this introduction comes from Barilli. In his review of *I racconti*, Barilli predictably criticizes the *author*. Calvino's use of "denotative" language "in cui ogni parola istituisce un puntuale e pulito rapporto con una cosa" (in which every word establishes a prompt and clean relation to a thing), Calvino's "misura classica" (his moderation), and his "Italian good sense" are recurring weaknesses characteristic of Calvino's style, discernible—according to Barilli—in this collection as well as in preceding works.[6] Calvino's style can be characterized by his "sguardo" (gaze), a sort of "innocent," "photographic" method of description which does not invest the text with any redeeming meaning or intensity.

> Lo squardo o il naturalistico fervore associativo di Calvino mancano infatti assolutamente di peso drammatico e patetico, si svolgono a un livello in cui le passioni quasi non giungono, o pervengono filtrate e depurate.[7]

> Calvino's gaze and his associative naturalistic fervor are completely devoid, in fact, of dramatic and emotional weight; they develop on a level which passions almost don't reach, or if they do, they arrive filtered and purified.

"La notomizzazione di Calvino, quindi, non va oltre le ambizioni e le possibilità di un gioco marginale . . . incapace di caricarsi di più alti valori" (Calvino's dissection, therefore, does not go beyond the ambitions and possibilities of an unimportant game . . . unable to become charged with higher values).[8] Barilli uses several examples from *Gli amori difficili* to illustrate his point. He says that the narrative techniques of the "Avventura di un viaggiatore" never "rise to the level of drama."[9] Then, later, he states that this lack of drama is underscored by the "asexuality" of the *Racconti*, and although Barilli acknowledges that sexual gestures and motivations *are* minutely recorded in the "Avventura di un soldato," they are rendered with "superior detachment and amusement." Once again "le cose [sono] le vere dominatrici della narrativa di Calvino" and "le implicazioni sessuali . . . si trovano in posizione subordinata rispetto ad esse" (things [are] what really dominate in Calvino's narrative—sexual implications . . . are in a subordinate position in respect to them).[10]

The following observation from the 1970 "Nota introduttiva" contrasts Barilli's position:

> La poetica *visiva* di questi racconti . . . "atto di impegno saltuario" [i.e., Barilli's "sguardo"] viene considerata invece l'essenza stilistica e anche morale dell'opera di Calvino da Francois Wahl. (Calvino, *Gli amori difficili*, p. xv)

> The visual poetics of these stories . . . "an act of desultory commitment" [i.e., Barilli's "gaze"] is considered instead the stylistic as well as moral essence of Calvino's work by Francois Wahl.

(We recall that Calvino's constant ideal of "morale" is closely linked to, and reflected in, his "stile," as he reiterates, as late as

1985, in the Corti interview mentioned in our Introduction). Wahl has determined the "sguardo" to be positive by attributing it not to the *narrator*, but to the *characters* in *Gli amori difficili*, who use it as a sort of refuge from their absurd situations.

In Friedman's study of this text we see the transformation of another Barilli "negative" into a positive aspect. Friedman believes that "love is expressed through a whole range of objects: a bed, a camera, books, eyeglasses, and more."[11] Although this does redeem Calvino's text from Barilli's condemnation, it is also a problematic oversimplification of the idea of love presented in the stories. At times, in fact—and as Friedman herself proves, in contradiction to her own statement—the object can provide a barrier, as in the case of the myopic protagonist for whom glasses aid in the "rediscover[y]" of "his long-lost love" while at the same time creating an obstacle to her recognization of him (or at least, so he explains her lack of recognition to himself).[12]

Ricci's perspective is neither to view the love stories as positive attempts at communication by the characters, nor as a failure of the author; neither does he perceive the characters to be coping adequately with difficult, "absurd" situations. Ricci says of the characters of *Gli amori difficili* and *La vita difficile*:

> The self, now fearful of the Other and of becoming engulfed in any relationship, creates a false self to deal with the insidiously dreadful world. They thus remain virtually undefined as characters, uncommitted and detached from any redeeming values, their absurdist stance and petty foibles allowing neither transcendence nor dramatic presence within the realms they inhabit.[13]

In another article, implementing the theories on schizophrenia expounded by R. D. Laing (*The Divided Self*), Ricci gives a reading of *Gli amori difficili* in which almost every protagonist "consciously retreats into a non-participatory observation of the transactions of the self in relation with outside reality."[14] The reality, Ricci affirms, is "an industrial society in the process of dissolution."[15]

> The protagonist is usually portrayed as exhibiting an attitude of volatile anxiety, and is withdrawn and conspicuously maladjusted. The self, fearful of the Other and of becoming engulfed in any relationship, often creates a false self which manages dealings with an insidiously dreadful world. This new and false self "is related primarily to objects of its own phantasies."[16]

Ricci's reading is based on the theories of Laing and A. Wilden. "A graphic illustration of this loss of self is provided by 'L'avventura di un soldato'," Ricci writes. The soldier, he feels, has become separated from his body, and views it as if from the outside.[17] For Ricci, the characters, not the author, are the ones unable to invest their reality with transcendent meaning.

We would like to posit a different view that validates both author and characters at one and the same time. We have seen repeatedly that love is essential to the development of self while at the same time it can jeopardize the very sense of self. We would like to thus validate the importance of the "self-referentiality" of the individual, which Ricci sees as an exceedingly negative and dangerous imprisonment of self within the self and an inability to communicate.

Friedman has noted that physical "movement" is one of the unifying characteristics of the stories. Almost every story involves movement in this literal sense, but also in the figurative connotation of a spiritual journey, an internal movement. As the "Nota introduttiva" states, almost every adventure "indica soltanto un movimento interiore, la storia d'uno stato d'animo, un itinerario verso il silenzio" (indicates only an internal movement, the story of a frame of mind, an itinerary toward silence— p. ix). This does not signify for us a defect of the character (or author), but rather the "subjectivity" of the "lover" (lover used in the broadest sense). As others have put it, it indicates the "sguardo," "the point of view,"[18] in the (usually male) protagonist's experience of love and *perception* of the other. As in "La spirale" and "Priscilla," we never follow a relationship between two lovers; we see *one lover's perception of that relationship* or *a lover's particular expression of love* and the realization that lover achieves within the "minor key" of the very internal, very personal experience that love is for that character. We see the impact of "love perceived" on the self; we see the self's perception of love. Each story, for us, is quite simply an odyssey into a particular "subjective" experience of eros and thus each shows another way of living human sexuality, another expression of human sexuality, lived entirely within the innermost recesses of the self.[19] Calvino does not explore erotic *interplay*, but the psychological aspects of sexuality. In such a way, far from being "asexual," as Barilli has claimed, the stories of *Gli amori difficili* extend the boundaries of the erotic once again (in a way different from *Le cosmicomiche*) to encompass many aspects of human experience. Calvino, in the many love stories he has written, has for the most part abstained from representing the sexual act per se, perhaps because of his rejection of the "mimesi decadentistica delle sensazioni."[20] He has also, as Falaschi has suggested, rejected the "neorealist" code for describing love scenes and erotic sentiment. So, although Calvino makes repeated use, as Friedman indicates, of the very traditional narrative theme of *love*, he seeks often to illuminate a new dimension of it, a different way in which love might be experienced. In light of his essays on sex and sexual representation, we might say that this ideological position is part of his "moral option." It is a way of rendering positively a subject that, in his opinion, defies direct representation and has more successfully in recent decades been treated negatively rather than positively in art, and has been overmysticized by the mass media. *Gli amori difficili* is yet another way of grappling with the representation of the erotic force.

Gli amori difficili is usually considered one of Calvino's "realistic" creations, in opposition to his "fantastic" writings.[21] Friedman asserts:

> The stories of *Gli amori difficili* are realistic; there is nothing unusual or supernatural about them, there is nothing anachronistic or odd about the world the characters live in or the actions they do, rather, they are extremely ordinary, at times even mundane [sic].[22]

However, the stories are not simply "slices of life." One might say that the melding of fantasy and reality which some critics attribute to Calvino's fiction occurs here as well. The settings are modern and familiar, the characters ordinary and "bourgeois" for the most part, but the stories are not entirely realistic. Yet they cannot be considered fantastic as it has been understood in *I nostri antenati* and *Le cosmicomiche*. For example, in the very first story, "L'avventura di un soldato," the characters and settings are familiar, almost generic: a train compartment, a soldier, a widowed matron from the provinces. Yet, because of the extreme impenetrability of the matron, to the reader as well as to the soldier (who never knows to the end whether his advances are welcome or not), the story can be interpreted, as we will see, as the fulfillment of a sexual fantasy as well as a sort of sexual bildungsroman. Ricci himself suggests that the episode may have been—as he puts it—"fictitious."[23] The second tale, "L'avventura di un bandito," may appear the least "realistic," as it is a "picaresque" view of the underworld. The third, "L'avventura di una bagnante," perhaps the most verisimilar so far (the loss of one piece of a flimsy bathing costume is a common enough experience on a beach), achieves nightmare proportions for the middle-class housewife who is the victim. A hint of this appears on the very first page when Isotta turns her face to the water "con un gesto come chi strofina le palpebre e le tempie contro il lenzuolo o il guanciale per ricacciare le lacrime chiamate da un pensiero notturno" (with a gesture like that of someone who rubs her eyes and her temples against the sheet and the pillow to drive back the tears triggered by a nocturnal thought—p. 19); the tear-provoking "pensiero notturno" suggests a nightmare. The experience reveals at the same time the matron's strange, inadmissible desires, as if the nightmare were threaded through with fantasy. (Or is this a fantasy turned nightmare to be acceptable?) To give yet another example, in the subsequent story, "L'avventura di un impiegato," Enrico Gnei, who has not slept at all the previous night because he has spent it making love with an enchanting "lady," finds that this lack of sleep gives him "come una innaturale lucidezza" (an unnatural lucidity)—the sleeplessness that brings on a certain hallucinatory effect. Such dreamlike atmospheres afford the reader a glimpse into the secret desires and fears of the protagonists.

To begin our analysis: the soldier in the first story is on an internal adventure that can be interpreted both as a sexual fantasy and a sexual bildungsroman. The trip seems to be crucial to Tomagra's sense of self, to his self-confidence, which we find to be very low throughout the story. The "conquest," the slow foreplay which Tomagra painstakingly and fearfully executes, seems integral to the growth of his sexual self, as well as an expression of that self. Throughout the tale, we are aware of his feelings of isolation and unworthiness as a soldier. Already by the end of the first paragraph Tomagra describes himself as having a coarse appearance and when the widow chooses to sit beside him he immediately and self-deprecatingly decides that it must be in order to travel more comfortably, to ride facing forward or to avoid drafts of air. The woman appears to Tomagra to be of magnificent proportions, a "sphinx" (p. 9). Tomagra's perception of her size, magnificence, dignity and inscrutability makes her a daunting prospect, a force to be reckoned with. That is, the more formidable she is, the more daring the adventure for the "unworthy" and "undeserving" soldier. Consequently, the more triumphant, the more satisfactory, the ultimate sexual experience. Tomagra's sense of self-confidence grows proportionately to the size of the task he has set before him.

Ahern claims: "When the two silently make love at the end of the tale, Tomagra comically believes that he has seduced the widow, although the opposite is true."[24] Friedman seems to agree that

> the whole seduction has been foreseen, and even orchestrated by the widow all along. The widow herself, from a desire to break out of her object-like state, but unable to do so, allows the soldier to seduce her, thus enabling her to make contact and become human.[25]

Although it strikes us that the widow—probably quite deliberately, as we will see—never becomes human, these critics' conviction presumably arises from the phrase "ogni cosa pareva in qualche modo da lei prevista" (everything seemed in some way foreseen by her—p. 12). But this could simply refer to the fact that nothing surprises her, that nothing at all seems to elicit a response from her. In fact, at the heart of Tomagra's attempt to communicate to her his desire is an absence of clearly decipherable messages, especially from her. Tomagra's curiously soldier-like "advances and retreats," his forays, are so timid, especially at the beginning, that they may hardly be construed as messages of desire to the widow. Even when he is sure he has given her a definite message by touching her through his pocket and has therefore succeeded in banishing all doubts, he realizes that even *this* gesture can be interpreted as a rummaging in his pocket for his train ticket.

Neither the reader nor Tomagra has any clear indication that the widow responds to him. Every gesture she makes, with her jacket for example, can be construed as encouragement or not. When her jacket spills over her lap, Tomagra asks: "Per offrigli un riparo o per sbarrargli il varco?" (To offer him shelter or to block his passage?—p. 9). From the beginning, she is inscrutable, her "sguardo" "irraggiungibile" (gaze unreachable—p. 5). Even by the end, she is "la vedova impassibile" (the impassive widow—p. 12). Yet, the few times she actually does make a gesture, Tomagra recoils. When she pulls her veil over her hat, Tomagra draws back in alarm and pretends to sleep, "perdendo così forse l'occasione di cogliere nel primo lampo del suo sguardo una risposta ai propri estremi dubbi" (in this way losing perhaps the opportunity to catch in the first flash of her gaze an answer to his own extreme doubts—p. 9). When, in the darkness of the tunnel, she inexplicably pushes him away, he scurries into his corner and wrings his hands. Tomagra actually seems to need her absence of response, to be able to view her only as the object of his desire, in order for him to proceed. His struggle is with the expression of his own sexuality, his own desire. The tunnel, in fact, evocative of a brief descent into the underworld in a minor key, increases the tone of "odyssey"; the train provides the literal odyssey which parallels the soldier's psychological journey. It is under the cover of this darkness in fact that he is able to touch her breasts, and, shortly thereafter when the compartment empties, he will have found the courage to satisfy his desire for the (sleeping?) widow.

Clearly, it is impossible to know the widow's thoughts, to understand her desires, to ascertain that she willed or wanted the seduction. It is impossible to "read" her, simply because the author did not want her to be "read." Perhaps he wished that the story might focus on the sexual and personal conquest which comprises the young soldier's growth. One indication of this is the fact that a description which strongly humanized the widow was edited out after the initial printing. In fact, many *Ultimo viene il corvo* editions that have 1949 as the copyright date differ from the original printing. Calvino deleted a long section describing the stockings and garters of the widow and the moving effect that these have on the soldier. Some of that long, omitted passage reads:

> Era, questo degli elastici, un segreto così teneramente bambino in una donna tanto grande e fiera, che Tomagra ne fu commosso, e in quel momento lei davvero si rimpicciolì al suo sguardo, e a lui prese una sorta di compassione affettuosa, una pietà furiosa.[26]

> This thing of the elastics was a secret so sweetly childlike in a woman so large and proud that Tomagra was moved by it, and in that moment she really did shrink in his eyes, and a sort of affectionate compassion, an intense pity, took hold of him.

In this omitted passage, Tomagra discerns her "pudica, fanciul-lesca fiducia" (chaste, girlish trust) in him. Certainly, this passage, had it been retained, would have assigned some very human qualities to the widow, would have made her far more accessible to the soldier, and would have established his ability to *read her*. Calvino may have chosen to eliminate these passages so that the widow would more than anything be a mirror for the soldier's desire, and for his journey into sexual development. In the end, in fact, Tomagra is amazed at his own accomplishments, awed that he had "osato tanto" (dared so much—Calvino, *Ultimo viene il corvo*, p. 12).

As for the importance of this sexual episode in Calvino's theory on sexuality, we see that he is investing the most minute movement of Tomagra's hand with the suspense and sensitivity of an erotic seduction, while omitting (from this final edition) some of the more explicit references to parts of clothing or parts of the body. The hand becomes totally invested with the intensity of the eros, responsible for the execution and reception of erotic sensation. The hand explores. One might say that Tomagra invests his movements with a sense of the wonder of what he is doing. Also, it is interesting that part of Tomagra's conquest is the elimination of a taboo. She is the inaccessible mystery, the sacred territory of sexuality; she represents the erotic to Tomagra, and at one point he thinks, "non poteva esserci ormai nulla di proibito, tra loro" (There could no longer be anything forbidden between them—p. 11).[27] Finally, one might go so far as to suggest that Tomagra's hand, and its circuitousness, reflect Calvino's notion of a circumlocutory approach to the portrayal of sexual encounter.

While this first story is clearly erotic in subject matter, "L'avventura di una bagnante" is more of a puzzle. Why is this tale included in this series? The female protagonist's mishap seems to have very little to do with the development of a love story. However, if we posit the centrality of the self on a backdrop of eroticism as an essential core of *Gli amori difficili*, then we recognize that the difficulties the protagonist undergoes pertain to her ability—or inability—to love her own body. If the search for love in Calvino becomes inextricably interwoven with internal plenitude, a sense of fulfillment, we see that the married woman Isotta, deprived of her social armor, which ironically consists of one flimsy little piece of bathing costume, sees herself in a position of extreme vulnerability in relation to the society around her as well as in relation to her own body. And, if we compare her to two other female protagonists in the text who literally undress in public, i.e., the poet's lover Delia and the reader's nameless lover, we see that these women seem to have a different relationship to their bodies.[28] Certainly, neither find themselves naked amongst strangers, but the reader and his lover—and one could argue that they are in essence strangers who have just met—make love naked on the rocks. Delia plunges into the water exuberantly, unembarrassed and unself-conscious under her lover's gaze. The comparison between Isotta's view of her naked body and another female protagonist's is made by Isotta herself much later when she notices a young woman who is probably heading out for some nude sunbathing:

> Passò pure una bionda abbronzata sola in sandolino, piena di sufficienza e d'egoismo, e certo andava al largo per far la cura del sole tutta nuda, e nemmeno le sfiorava il pensiero che quella nudità potesse essere una disgrazia o una condanna. (Calvino, *Gli amori difficili*, p. 23)

> A tanned blonde went by, alone in her canoe, self-sufficient and self-contained, and certainly she was heading far out to sunbathe in the nude, and the idea that such nudity could be a disgrace or a sentence did not even cross her mind.

Unlike these protagonists, Isotta is incredibly self-conscious and helpless. The description of the loss of *lo slip*, the bottom half of the bikini, in the second sentence of the story as "un fatto senza rimedio" (an irremediable fact) highlights her helplessness and the sense of panic which the plot elaborates (p. 19). Her self-consciousness, her discomfort which grows into distress, is apparent from the moment she appears on the beach for the first time in a bikini among so many strangers.

Isotta, by wearing so little in public, seems to feel that she is doing something taboo, something in some way daring and even wicked. She thinks that she may, in her bikini, appear "sportiva, o molto alla moda, mentre lei in realtà era una signora davvero alla buona e casalinga" (sporty, or very fashionable, whereas in reality she was an unassuming woman and housewife—p. 20). She associates the bikini with a certain sinfulness, one might say, a certain modernity; it is a sort of symbol of "modern values" with which Isotta certainly does not associate herself, and of which perhaps she disapproves. She seems to feel she is violating certain social codes, and in this sense may feel she is breaking some newly breakable taboo. (It seems that bikinis first appeared in 1946, five years before this story was written.)[29] However, her public nudity violates social taboos, and therefore precipitates her into a—to the reader—illuminating crisis.

The description of the woman's perception of her own body recalls the words of Calvino in his 1961 essay on sex and its representation: "siamo più lontani che mai da una felicità naturale" (we are farther than ever from a natural happiness).[30] Isotta sees that her body is clearly visible under the sheen of the water and twists and turns to observe it. She finds that "sempre quest'offensivo nudo corpo le veniva dietro. Era una fuga dal suo corpo, che lei stava tentando" (this offensive body always followed her. It was an escape from her body that she was attempting—p. 21). She thinks, "Eppure questo corpo . . . era ben stato una sua gloria . . . Oppure no" (And yet this body had once been her pride and glory . . . Or maybe not—p. 21). She realizes that perhaps her identity hinged on her image as "signora vestita" and her "nudità le apparteneva così poco, era un inconsulto stato della natura" (nudity was so little a part of her, it was an ill-advised state of nature—p. 21). She is torn between pride for her body, and shame for its nakedness. "Ad avere un corpo la signora s'era abituata con un po' di riluttanza, dopo i primi delusi anni romantici" (The woman had gotten used to her body somewhat reluctantly, after the first disillusioned romantic years—p. 21). This last observation implies that her expectations of sex were very different from her actual experience, suggesting perhaps one of the dangers of the "mythicized" perception of sex. Isotta is, by her nudity, physically alienated from other swimmers and sexually alienated from herself. Having stepped out of the bounds of "housewifely" codes of behavior, she finds herself totally isolated and unable to cope.

She flees bathers and boaters, and seems a bit like a character out of a medieval depiction of the Expulsion from the Garden, à la Massaccio. Her nude body grows suddenly to huge proportions in her awareness, becomes central to her focus, and, she is sure, central to everyone else's focus as well. Men of all ages occupied in various activities—swimming, fishing—appear to be pointing to her significantly, lewdly, or circling around her. She suspects that "ognuno di questi uomini da anni fantasticasse d'una donna cui doveva capitare quel ch'era capitato a lei, e passasse le estati al mare sperando d'esser lì al momento buono" (each of these men for years fantasized about a woman to whom would happen what had happened to her, and spent the summers at sea hoping to be there at just the right moment—p. 22). Two things immediately surface from such an observation: first, the narcissism in which Isotta indulges demonstrates a sort of fantasy of her own as object and center of male sexual fantasy; second, that her body does not belong to her but to men. It is a sort of object. (The soldier too perceives the matron as "muto oggetto," p. 12). This agony of self-consciousness appears as a sort of dream of public nudity, which in Freudian terms might be interpreted as a sort of exhibitionism. Isotta seeks deliverance, perhaps from some lifeguard who must be "quasi angelico" (a reference meant to introduce religious notions of sin?). However, the sensuality ("the fleshy lips and sinewy muscles"—p. 22) of the lifeguard she does see terrifies her; so sure is she that she will excite irresistible desire in him that she feels she cannot trust him.

It does not occur to her to seek the help of other women, since with them she can only have a relationship of rivalry. It is interesting to note that in observing this, the narrator uses the phrase "nelle sue deluse fantasie" (in her disappointed fantasies), which corroborates our reading of Isotta's experience as revelatory of a sort of narcissistic fantasy. The adjective "deluse" implies that they may be incorrect perceptions, that she may be imagining things that aren't there. But to condemn her outright as some sort of psychologically unbalanced protagonist would be an exaggeration, because she is no less central to her fantasy than is the soldier to his. Certainly, in each individual's relationship to his/her own sexuality, such preoccupation with the self is typical, ordinary. The plentitude of self is necessary even if it may appear to outsiders as overblown and onanistic. However, it is true that Isotta indulges beyond plentitude in a sort of narcissism. Ahern also observes: "she is alienated from her body and her desires, despite her strong sensuality."[31] While we feel that this "strong sensuality" is not confirmed by the story, it is nonetheless true that—unlike the soldier, for example—Isotta never doubts her attractiveness to men, her desirability.

Isotta's anguish and shame cause her to stay in the water so long as to endanger her well-being, and she begins to blame the others—the strangers, the bathers—for her dilemma. When her saviors, a boy and a man, appear with a green skirt, after a moment of disorientation everything—the world around her—immediately settles into its appropriate dimensions and she within it. Once covered again, even the realization that these two men had seen her naked underwater does not upset her; she is happy "che ne avessero provato curiosità e piacere" (that they had derived curiosity and pleasure from it—p. 26).

The reader may question the purpose of the descriptions of domestic activity that follow. Perhaps they are proof that life has continued as usual, that people have been doing what they usually do, and now that Isotta is dressed she can appreciate that she is not central to their focus. The focus has shifted away from her. The men, women, and children involved in cooking, helping each other, sewing, etc., are a vision of the world set to rights again, a world unaffected by Isotta's crisis. The day had been proceeding in its "natural" order for everyone but Isotta.

In "L'avventura di una moglie," there are other elements common to this and other "avventure." The protagonist of the story is a young wife who has only been married a few years, but whose husband, like the bather's, is temporarily away. When they find themselves outside of the protective shell of the married unit, and so, in a sense, divested momentarily of their perhaps limiting but safe roles and identities as wives, they are left to explore their own identities. For Isotta, this means a great deal of anguish over her body, which, when taken out of the marriage bed, is burdensome to her. The reader, through her crisis, is able to discern much of the psychological elements of her makeup. For Stefania, however, being away from her husband means an opportunity for greater self-definition, for maturity, for adulthood. Like Isotta, Stefania breaks a sort of social taboo: she is out with old friends, drinking and dancing until the wee hours, and then spends the four hours between two and six in the morning with a young man, Fornero, while she waits for her building door to open, because she has forgotten her key. Such activities are taboo because they fall outside of unspoken social codes that discourage wives from socializing in the evenings with men not their husbands, and spending the nighttime hours with them. The fact that her adventure takes place entirely outside of her home underlines her position outside the boundaries of social codes.

"L'avventura" itself may appear to consist entirely of the "adulterio" of simply spending the nighttime hours with another man, with whom Stefania is a little in love—but so little that she has forgotten him by the time the door opens at the end of the story. However, the real adventure, like Isotta's and the soldier's, involves "internal movements." Stefania's adventure too promotes a state of self-love, a sort of awareness of "plentitude" and independence. Like the other protagonists, Stefania's adventure is with herself.

Like the *impiegato* of another eponymous adventure, she has not slept at all; so, as all the central characters we have discussed so far, she is in a strange state of mind. She finds that being by herself at that hour is rather exciting. Like the *impiegato*, she walks into an unfamiliar bar, for, like the *impiegato*, her life has taken a brief, unusual, and enjoyable turn. Stefania realizes that she does not need to explain herself to the bartender, that she doesn't need to account to anyone but herself. She orders self-confidently.

Stefania's story is among the least ambiguous in the collection. Ahern notes that "she discovers a new self-confidence, a capacity to deal with all kinds of men as an equal"[32] and Friedman comments on Stefania's newfound sense of "independence."[33] Her sense of plenitude, her growth, derives from the fact that, by breaking a sort of social code, by doing something taboo, she is testing her capacities beyond the role of wife protected by her husband. In fact, one might say that her sense of empowerment lies in her ability to reject the advances of the men around her, thereby preserving those "doveri coniugali" (conjugal duties) that she feared she was no longer honoring (p. 80), while still enjoying these men's company. Stefania rejects Fornero's insistent advances, evades the pursuit of the man in the blue suit, smilingly turns down the invitation of the young hunter, and refuses a drink with the "operaio." She has ventured outside of the territories society deemed (deems?) safe for a wife and yet has managed to preserve her sense of values—and enjoy herself—nonetheless. The adventure is her own becoming. She is, like Qfwfq the cell and Qfwfq the mollusk, like the soldier at the end of his adventure and Isotta in the water, a little in love with herself, a state which allows her to enjoy the world around her.

In the same way that the narrative structures and plots of the adventures of the two wives can be compared and contrasted, so—as we suggested earlier—can the adventures of Stefania and the *impiegato*, Enrico, both of whom spend the night out, and confront a morning world not part of their daily routine. Friedman, who rapidly compares the two protagonists' experiences, notes that, unlike the wife, Enrico is free "to spend the night with whom he chooses,"[34] and, again unlike Stefania, he wishes to share his experience with someone.[35] One might also say that Stefania slowly acquires a consciousness of plenitude, a pride in being alone and totally herself, that Gnei by the end must inevitably lose.

Enrico's adventures may, like Stefania's "adultery," be his night of love, but perhaps, more accurately, his real adventure is the clash of cold light of morning with his night's experience, a clash that offers him certain realizations. The Enrico that waltzes down the hill from his tryst relishes his own plenitude, his very sense of self. Like the soldier, the traveler, and the poet, he feels enormously fortunate to have been the recipient of the erotic experience granted by the woman. Enrico relishes his very mediocrity (as we will see), a mediocrity that is paradoxically both undermined and reinforced by the fact that Gnei is convinced that the unexpected success of the previous night was coincidental, and owed nothing to any personal charm he might have exercised. The fact that the "lady" is of a higher social class than he, and that her house is on a hill, which symbolically further indicates her superiority, makes him feel special while reinforcing his mediocrity in relation to her. Yet his "good fortune" renders him particularly self-satisfied, and in a sense invalidates his self-proclaimed mediocrity, or makes it a necessary part of his own distinguishing features. Gnei is convinced, in fact, that "solo la sua apparenza discreta e un po' anonima . . . lo poteva designare come compagno non impegnativo o vistoso" (only his discreet and somewhat anonymous appearance . . . could single him out as a companion who would not be too demanding or obtrusive— p. 27). It is the clash, however, between his own ordinary life "da impiegato" and the transcendent erotic experience of the preceding night that sets his routine askew; the erotic experience, however, can have no real space within his morning's self-contained routine. The descent from the hill also symbolically signals the descent from the erotic into the mundane, from the unique to the routine, from sexual euphoria to its slow dissipation.

The incongruity between the extraordinary impact of the erotic experience and the routine by which Gnei defines his life is evinced in his decision not to return home to change his clothing, "perché lo prese il timore che la casa, la ripetizione di gesti quotidiani dissolvessero l'atmosfera di straordinarietà e ricchezza in cui si muoveva" (because a fear took hold of him that the house, the repitition of everyday gestures would dissolve the rich and extraordinary atmosphere in which he moved—p. 28). Yet there are many indications throughout the tale that Gnei has orchestrated his life to a certain subdued tenor: his own description of himself as nondescript; his happiness that his experience was none other than a one-night stand, because he has no room in his life for love, because "una relazione continuata avrebbe comportata problemi troppo imbarazzanti per il suo tenore di vita abituale" (a continuing relationship would have involved problems too embarrassing for his usual tenor of life—p. 27); the fact that he is a methodical person; the fact that he is a careful, systematic reader who reads a paper from start to finish; and the "trasporto amoroso" he feels for his own mundane, bureaucratic job.

There are other indications, though, that he is exceedingly self-satisfied and self-contained. He says he is modest by nature, but perceives himself to be a mysterious but happy stranger to the early morning tram riders; he is full of himself and feels that "era un uomo che guarda i glicini da uomo che sa guardare i glicini; era conscio di questo, Enrico Gnei" (he was a man who looks at wistaria like a man who knows how to look at wistaria; this was what Enrico Gnei was conscious of—p. 28); his "umiltà istintiva" makes him feel sorry for his married friend, Bardetta, which translates merely to a feeling of superiority over him (p. 31). (Only later does he realize that he may be underestimating his old friend!) So, this tension in his personality, this coexistence of mediocrity as both Gnei's self-expression as well as his imprisonment, also somehow amounts to a sort of belief in his own *individuality*.

Gnei descends the hill a little enamored of the benevolent and generous lady, and perhaps a lot in love with himself and with life in general. His erotic experience and his sense of plenitude have fused to give him a renewed sensual perception of the world around him: "Un muovere di vento, un ronzio, un odore d'alberi gli parevano cose di cui dovesse in qualche modo impossessarsi e godere; e non si riaddattava a modi di gustare la bellezza più discreti" (The movement of the wind, the buzzing, the smell of trees seemed to him things which he should somehow try to possess and enjoy; and he couldn't get reaccustomed to more moderate ways of savouring beauty—p. 27). In a burst of uncharacteristic spontaneity, he breezes onto the tram and sits down in a disorderly way, but then pulls himself together. His heightened awareness of self and Other and world is perhaps a common effect of his pleasurable experience, a reaction with which many readers may empathize. To read these characters as social misfits undermines the very ordinariness that they—and perhaps Calvino too (in the "Nota introduttiva")—project, as well as the empathetic (as well as ironic) connection between reader and character that the author may have been trying to create. Many elect to live their lives in the predictable, self-contained way that Gnei chooses.

Gnei's morning adventure is the process by which he tries to keep alive the night's amorous adventure, especially in his memory. He seeks to establish some tangible record of his night's adventure and the wonderful ultrabright sheen the world has acquired. He is trying in some way to retain his sense of "inna-moramento," of the erotic connection with life he has discovered. He tries to do this by expressing his "euforia" (Calvino, *Gli amori difficili*, p. 31) and repeatedly fails. His communication needs are complex: on one level, he has a simple need to express, "esprimere"; he also needs to confide in Bardetta in order that that night might "lasciare un segno, assumere un significato definitivo, invece di sparire come sabbia in un mare di giorni vuoti e uguali" (leave a sign, acquire a definite meaning, instead of disappearing like sand in a sea of empty, identical days—p. 32); and, finally, he needs to keep the experience alive:

> "Questo è il segreto . . . che in ogni momento, in ogni cosa che io faccio o dico, sia implicito tutto quello che ho vissuto." Ma lo rodeva un'ansia . . . di non riuscire a esprimere, né con allusioni e men che meno con parole esplicite, e forse neppure col pensiero, la pienezza che sapeva d'aver raggiunto. (P. 33)

> "This is the secret . . . that in every moment, in everything I do and say, all that I have lived is implicit." But an anxiety gnawed at him . . . of being unable to express either by allusion and even less with explicit words, and maybe not even with his thoughts, the fullness he knew he had reached.

Gnei struggles with the difficulty of expressing his experience, of his sense of *pienezza*, which defies expression, and falls into the category of the "indicibile." "Ogni esperienza indicibile è subito perduta" (Every inexpressible [unsayable] experience is quickly lost), the "Nota introduttiva" says referring to this "adventure" (p. ix). We would like to point out that it does not say: "ogni esperienza non detta," (every unspoken experience) but "ogni esperienza indicibile"; it is not merely Gnei's difficulty in communication, noted by several critics, which we observed here, but the difficulty in communicating his sense of plenitude, as well as erotic experience, which Calvino addresses in his essays and exemplifies through his "Priscilla" story. As happened to Qfwfq the cell, even memory betrays Gnei in the end (p. 33). Gnei seems to discover, as did Qfwfq in his approximative uses of language, that it is impossible to give the "equivalent" of something "which goes too far beyond the word."[36] We will see this same foiled attempt to describe the indescribable in "L'avventura di un poeta," in our final discussion of *Gli amori difficili*.

While "L'avventura di un impiegato" depicts the sense of fullness that can accompany an erotic adventure, "L'avventura di un viaggiatore" explores the sense of fullness one traveler experiences in his anticipation of an amorous encounter. Federico the traveler enjoys that same sense of plenitude of which Gnei was aware. In the suspended period *after* Federico's hectic weekdays but *before* his encounter with Cinzia, Federico can savor the anticipation which is the beginning of his amorous adventure. "Al termine di un viaggio per raggiungere l'amante, un uomo capisce che la vera notte d'amore è quella che ha passato . . . correndo verso di lei" (At the end of a journey to his beloved, a man understands that the true night of love is the one he spent . . . running toward her—"Nota introduttiva," p. x). The train ride, which Federico has invested with great energy and ritual, is utilized as a form of self-expression. The desire he feels, the desire he savors and anticipates, is highly personal and integral to his enjoyment of himself. Let us briefly consider this other "innamoramento di sé."

Each minute detail of his trip, each obstacle, from the difficulty of changing a large bill to the lack of change at the newspaper stand, are regarded as welcome challenges to be overcome. The purchase of a second-class ticket gives him "il piacere del risparmio . . . la soddisfazione di mettere a frutto la propria esperienza, e un senso di libertà e larghezza nei gesti e nei pensieri" (the pleasure of saving . . . the satisfaction of using his experience, and a sense of freedom and spaciousness in his gestures and thoughts—p. 48). Like Gnei, Federico is self-contained, though his life, unlike Gnei's, seems to be one of frenetic confusion and movement (his life, we are told, is conditioned by others and directed outwardly). Love provides for him (as it did for Gnei) a contrasting experience: for Federico, the excitement of total control, of orchestration of ritual. "Federico tendeva incessantemente a difendere un proprio stato di concentrazione interiore" (Federico tended incessantly to preserve a state of internal concentration—p. 48) which he exercises during his trip. "In questo ['un rituale minuzioso'], appunto, consisteva l'arduo piacere dei suoi viaggi" (In this [detailed ritual] consisted, precisely, the arduous pleasure of his trips—p. 52). The trip becomes invested with his entire identity, and he fantasizes that the little pillow he buys is his daily letter to Cinzia: "e al posto della pagina di scrittura ansiosa era Federico in persona a prendere la via invisibile della posta notturna" (and in place of the page covered in anxious handwriting was Federico in person taking the invisible road of the night mail—p. 49). Like other Calvinian characters, he too is his own message.

This pillow represents and foreshadows the pleasures of the refreshing privacy of his rest on the train, as well as the intimacy that awaits him at his destination. Every point of his journey gives him pleasure. We note his sense of complacency: "il viaggio lo metteva in una condizione di spirito favorevole, una condizione propria anzi all'uomo maturo, all'uomo che sa il male e il bene della vita, ed ora si prepara a godere, meritatamente, il bene" (the trip put him in a favorable mood, a mood indeed characteristic of the mature man, of the man who knows the good and bad in life, and now gets ready to enjoy, deservedly, the good—p. 51). The adverb "meritatamente" underscores his perception of high self-worth. "In tutto l'universo lui e lui solo era l'uomo che correva verso Cinzia U." (In the whole universe he and he alone was the man running toward Cinzia U.—p. 55) and he is proud to be "volando tra le braccia d'una donna come Cinzia U." (flying into the arms of a woman like Cinzia U.—p. 51). The worth of the women increases the worth of the men who love them, for the soldier, Enrico and Federico. The rhetorical question, "poteva Federico chiedere di più dalla vita?" (what more could Federico ask of life?) recalls Gnei's conviction that "[lui] ha avuto quanto di meglio poteva desiderare al mondo" ([he] has had the best in the world that he could ask for—p. 27).

Federico goes to sleep, wakes up feeling cold and tries to recover the feeling of fullness—the same noun used to describe Gnei's state after his night's pleasure—that lulled him to sleep. In the end, at his destination, he falls into a hectic rhythm again, reminiscent perhaps of his hectic workdays, and almost loses that sense of plenitude:

> lui era già nella tensione dei loro giorni insieme, nell'affannosa guerra delle ore, e capiva che non sarebbe riuscito a dirle nulla di quel che era stata per lui quella notte, che già sentiva svanire, come ogni perfetta notte d'amore, al dirompere crudele dei giorni. (P. 58)

> he was already in the tension of their days together, in the wearisome war of the hours, and he understood that he would never succeed in telling her anything of what that night had been for him, that night that he already felt was vanishing, like every perfect night of love, in the cruel break of day.

Like Gnei, Federico will not be able to comunicate his sense of plenitude, his "innamoramento di sé" which affords him a full enjoyment of life's experiences and of his memory of her, as well as the full expression of his desire. His night vanishes as does

Gnei's, even though he has a lover with whom he might confide. But how does one explain that a night anticipating one's lover is a "perfect night of love"? It is again one of those "esperienze indicibili," a very personal expression and enjoyment of intimacy, love and the sensual. Something about such fullness is difficult to communicate, to represent, and perhaps even appears a little bit indecent, because it seems to border on narcissism. However, it also validates the self.

The protagonists of *Gli amori difficili* we have so far encountered are struggling against some sort of social taboo which makes a certain form of sexual expression, expression of the erotic, difficult. In his game of *ars combinatoria*, in his rearrangement of variables, Calvino gives us another rather ironic situation which shows the absence of sexual expression where it is most expected, where society sanctions it, in fact. In another reversal of the expected, another instance of "straniamento," Calvino portrays a married couple who *do not* make love, because the circumstances of their jobs thwart them.

In "L'avventura di due sposi," one of the most ironic and poignant of the tales, Elide works during the day and Arturo on the nightshift. Some of the poignancy of this tale derives from its complete accessibility to contemporary readers as a rather common and unremarkable effect of urbanization, here subjected to a close-up. The tale traces the two counterpointing rhythms of the couple's daily lives and some of the deliciously intimate moments of their brief encounters in their daily routine. For example, on the days her husband considerately wakes her with coffee in bed, Elide's stretching arms may end up around his neck. At the same time, the raincoat he still wears makes her speculate on the weather, which she will soon be braving as she makes her own way to work. The intimacy of their smooth bathroom-sharing rhythm might include a caress and an embrace, quickly cut short by Elide's awareness of the time. Their intimacy is further transmitted by Arturo's imagining his wife catching her bus; their very routine, the sharing of each in the other's routine, becomes a sort of expression of their union, the only expression for which they have time.

Certain aspects of their routine seem also to permit erotic indulgence, although in the "minor," attenuated note peculiar to the entire collection. The bed, in fact, seems to be the—ironic— center of this enjoyment, as we see from Arturo's enjoyment of the warmth on his wife's side and her lingering scent.

Habit and ritual have been recurring themes in this collection of stories; the protagonists' lives or their expressions of desire have been characterized not simply by an attention to detail on the part of the author, but rather by an attention to detail *as part of the protagonist's ritual or routine*. Ahern has rightly pointed out that no single generalization can be applied to all of the stories, such that, for example, we might say that Isotta's crisis grows out of a break from routine.[37] Yet the soldier's "seduction" of the widow underlines the ritualistic qualities of the act of love. The *impiegato* whose sense of self seems to derive from his regimented routine tries to imbue this routine with the sensual glow of his recent erotic experience. The *viaggiatore* experiences and expresses the essence of his desire in his own indulgence in routine: the more predictable the results of his planning, the more successful his planning, the greater the self-satisfaction. One might even view this portrayal of routine as a way of exploring the role of the erotic in daily life, something which Calvino claims in his two articles is almost impossible to portray. Calvino seems in some way to accomplish this, though, by staying away from a description of the actual act of love—a description which he usually gives in the most metaphoric or elliptical of terms on the few occasions he does focus on the actual act of consummation.[38] That is, Calvino seems to shift the lens, in a sort of "straniamento," to give yet another dimension of the expression of the erotic.

Arturo and Elide's separate yet married life is highly, almost rigidly, regulated by routine. Yet, in the commonplace and habitual—like their bathroom arrangement—we see their expression of love. For example, Arturo, who awaits Elide, makes some dinner, makes the bed, but all this is "una specie di rituale per aspettare lei, quasi un venirle incontro pur restando tra le pareti di casa" (a type of ritual for waiting for her, almost a way of going to meet her while staying within the walls of the house—p. 89). Like the *viaggiatore*, he seems to use the ritual as a way of *actively* waiting, of loving her even when she is not there, of expressing his love for her.

Ironically, very soon after she appears, after the initial excitement of seeing her, Arturo is already mentally on his way to work. The counterpoint continues. He is rested; she is tired. She would like more attention; he is preparing for work. Then, at the dinner table, one of those poignant moments of intimacy:

> allora c'era il momento dello struggimento che li pigliava tutti e due d'avere così poco tempo per stare insieme, e quasi non riuscivano a

portarsi il cucchiaio alla bocca, dalla voglia che avevano di star lì a tenersi per mano. (P. 89)

Then came the moment of torment that took hold of both of them of having so little time to be together, and they almost couldn't get their spoons to their mouths, they were so overcome by the desire to stay where they were holding hands.

This is the one moment in which their routines are in sync, and ironically though understandably, their separateness is all they can think about. The moment is too brief, but as Arturo gives his wife a good-bye hug, it seems to him that "solo allora capisse com'era morbida e tiepida la sua sposa" (only then did he understand how soft and warm his wife was—pp. 89–90). Her warmth, which has characterized her lingering presence in the bed, seems here a delicious temptation. It stands in contrast to the cold he must soon weather and the cold house in the morning. Her warmth is an erotic inducement, symbolic of the dimensions of their intimacy. Once in bed, Elide sticks out a foot, testing her husband's side of the bed for "il calore di lui" (the warmth of him—p. 90). However, it is on her side that they in some sense are united; through the warmth that they leave for each other on the same side of the bed, they express their love. In any other case, this warmth would be a merely commonplace image, but here, having attained significance as their only point of contact in bed, it becomes an erotic expression (if we include all aspects of desire and love in the force that is eros) while retaining its ordinariness and accessibility.

These two characters are wrapped up in the demands of their very separate lives. Their separation is determined by the clock. In a certain sense, even their expression of affection and desire is lived separately in silence—in their enjoyment of the warmth the other leaves in their "unused" matrimonial bed. The enjoyment of the erotic in *Gli amori difficili*, it seems, is a very solitary, personal, subjective experience, for a variety of reasons, as we have seen.

The last adventure to be analyzed ended *Gli amori difficili* as it appeared in the *Racconti* and offers the greatest possibilities for plumbing the phenomenon of "silence," which has been one of the most intriguing themes of *Gli amori* for the few critics who have turned their attention to it since the 1970 "Nota introduttiva."[39] Silence may be considered the consequence of the difficulty in human communication that has been one of the

great themes of the twentieth century. It is a consequence of
the troubles individuals face in understanding each other. De
Lauretis, using *Gli amori difficili* as a starting point, writes:
"This core of silence at the bottom of human communication is
an area of passivity, a non-disposable residue of negativity that,
for Calvino, is the essence of the sexual relationship. Desire
is founded in absence."[40] In fact, the 1970 "Nota introduttiva"
says that at the heart of these stories is "la difficoltà di
comunicazione, una zona di silenzio al fondo dei rapporti
umani" (a difficulty in communicating, an area of silence at the
heart of human relations—Calvino, *Gli amori difficili*, p. ix).
Even the title, "Adventures," is ironic, because "nella maggior
parte dei casi indica soltanto un movimento interiore, la storia
d'uno stato d'animo, un itinerario verso il silenzio" (in most cases
it indicates only an internal movement, the story of a frame of
mind, an itinerary toward silence—p. ix).

However, silence may be more complex than an *a priori* to
love, as the inevitable failure of love. Love has been shown—e.g.,
in *Le cosmicomiche*—to be very positive. For example, silence
may also result from the ultimate, unique subjectivity of the experience—the individual perceptions—that renders it difficult
to relate. On the other hand, the theme of silence in *Gli amori
difficili* may also be closely linked to Calvino's theories on language, and on erotic language. In the "Nota introduttiva," we
read:

> Va detto che per Calvino questo nucleo di silenzio non è soltanto un
> passivo ineliminabile in ogni rapport umano: racchiude pure un va-
> lore prezioso, assoluto. "E nel cuore di questo sole era silenzio," è
> detto nell' *Avventura di un poeta*, un racconto dove la scrittura, fin
> tanto che evoca immagini di bellezza e felicità, è rarefatta laconica
> pausata, ma appena deve dire la durezza della vita si fa minuziosa,
> copiosa, fitta fitta. (Calvino, *Gli amori difficili*, p. ix)

> It must be said that for Calvino this nucelus of silence is not just
> a state of passivity which cannot be eliminated from any human
> relationship: it also embraces a precious and absolute value. "And
> in the heart of this sun was silence," it is said in the *Avventura di
> un poeta*, a story in which the writing, as long as it evokes images
> of beauty and happiness, is rarified, laconic, full of pauses, but as
> soon as it must talk about life's hardships it becomes meticulous,
> copious, very dense.

In this typically ambiguous remark, we are told that silence does not merely constitute a negative, but may also refer to something positive, in so far as it contains a "precious and absolute value." Silence, in Calvino's 1961 essay on sexual representation, was posited as a solution to the difficulties in representing the erotic in that social and artistic context. We recall that Calvino felt that to say nothing, to choose not to represent the erotic, to exclude it from one's fiction, presented perhaps the best "moral option," given the difficulties in portraying the erotic positively. "L'avventura di un poeta," written only a few years before the publication of the 1961 article, may reflect some of these ideas, for the figure of the poet may be viewed as Calvino's alter ego. In his struggle between silence and expression, Calvino, we remember, advocated precision in language, but acknowledged the erotic as one of those "inexpressible" human experiences. Nonetheless, language for Calvino must seek to redeem experience from the strictures of taboo and struggle to say the unsayable. Yet, paradoxically, in the 1961 essay, silence was considered by Calvino as the modesty of the word when faced by experiences that are beyond its abilities. This artistic dilemma between respect for "sacred" experiences that also elude representation and the battle of language to say something, recurs throughout his work, and is especially evident in dealing with erotic themes. In the poet's adventure, the author seems to give us a better idea of the struggle between experience and its expression, and the refusal to use words "by now worn and useless" for the erotic and other precious experience.[41]

The poet and his lover Delia H. are exploring a very small island along the coastal waters of a relatively undeveloped area of southern Italy. The scene is idyllic and intimate: amidst silence, he rows the boat as she sunbathes. When his ears perk up, she asks what he hears. He hears silence, but this silence is an active thing, rather than an absence of sound. "Le isole hanno un silenzio che si sente" (The islands have a silence one can hear—p. 91), he says. Silence is made up of the minutest sounds, and the silence of the island is different from the silence of the sea, the narrative tells us. Yet this description of silence evokes poetically and effectively the very things it does not describe.

Ironically, the poet—master of words—is faced with silence, both the active silence comprised of natural sounds and his own inability to participate in, and add to, Delia's verbal transports of joy over the natural beauty they encounter. In fact, Delia perceives his silence as reluctance to participate, as if words were the medium not simply of transmitting her rapture but consequently of experiencing it more fully. The poet, however, is at a loss for words. Like the "parole logore e inservibili" that describe the erotic, words which Calvino says become worn out in a few years,[42] the poet is "diffidente (per natura e per educazione letteraria) verso le emozioni e le parole già fatte proprie da altri . . . La felicità era per Usnelli uno stato sospeso, da vivere trattenendo il fiato" (diffident by nature and literary background toward emotions and words already appropriated by others . . . Happiness for Usnelli was a suspended state, to be lived while holding one's breath—pp. 91–92).

Usnelli's reaction as a writer to the wonder all around him, to the happiness that he feels, is to hold his breath—not to speak. The reader suspects that Usnelli feels words might be inadequate, and might in some way violate this sense of wonder, especially words that have become clichéd and have therefore lost their ability to render the impact and wonder they are trying to convey. Usnelli rejects trite words. Instead, he looks to the skyline, the horizon—symbol here of limitations—for an opening, an end to the limitations, perhaps "un pianeta diverso o una parola diversa" (a new planet or a new word—p. 92). The new word will bring a new planet, a new way of seeing things, a new way of expressing things.

Usnelli grows uncomfortable. "Era nervoso. Il suo pensiero, abituato a tradurre le sensazioni in parole . . . adesso niente, non riusciva a formularne neanche una" (He was nervous. His thoughts, used to translating sensations into words . . . now there was nothing, he couldn't even formulate one—p. 92). In the grotto, Delia tests the echo, cries out, recites poetry and invites her lover to express himself. But he lacks her genuine spontaneity, and is mistrustful of words that might banalize his experience.

When Delia decides to swim, he is "sempre a fiato sospeso. Per lui, essere innamorato di Delia era stato sempre così, come nello specchio di questa grotta: essere entrato in un mondo al di là della parola" (continuing to hold his breath. For him, being in love with Delia had always been like this, like in the mirror of this cave: to have entered a world that goes beyond the word—p. 93). These words are exactly those words that Calvino used in his 1969 article on sex and laughter when he said that humor might in fact be a sign of "the modesty of the word in the face of that which goes too far beyond the word [*al di là della parola*]" (p. 212, italics mine). In this adventure, silence replaces laughter as a reaction to that which goes beyond the word. Usnelli acknowledges, on the heels of this thought, that he has never written even *one* verse on love. Silence is his reaction to happiness, wonder, and love—positive human experiences.

Yet, though the poet Usnelli is struck dumb, the author Calvino is busily writing. Sometimes through the story the two seem to merge; in the end, for example, when confronted by a more squalid, darker human experience, Usnelli finds many words: "questa angoscia del mondo umano era il contrario di quella che gli comunicava poco prima la bellezza della natura: come là ogni parola veniva meno, così qua era una ressa di parole che gli si affollavano alla mente" (The anguish of the human world was the opposite of the one that the beauty of nature had earlier aroused in him: just as there every word failed, so here it was a swarm of words that crowded his mind—p. 94). The author in fact ends with a thicket of words and details, so that one might assume that he and Usnelli are at that point one.

However, earlier, when Usnelli wordlessly watches his lover swimming nude, the author does give a description, and we must wonder whether he describes what Usnelli sees, or whether in fact the author wishes us to view the words as Usnelli's words. A possible interpretation might be that Usnelli reflects, personifies, Calvino's conviction that wonder is ineffable and defies speech. However, Calvino himself *must* battle with words in order to describe the ineffable.

The description of Delia, naked and at one with the water, transforms her into a *creature* of natural beauty. She is serene, statuesque almost, and is compared to the sea animals: her body under the sea transmits the blue of a jellyfish. To describe her sex, the metaphor *star* is used and then eroticized by a suggestion of oral sex in the likening of the star to a "frutto marino." Her arched foot is likened to a small fish. Delia and the natural environment seem to work in a relationship of reciprocal eroticization.

Usnelli watches and understands "che quel che ora la vita dava a lui era qualcosa che non a tutti è dato di fissare a occhi aperti, come il cuore più abbagliante del sole" (what life was now giving him was not given to everyone to feast upon with open eyes, like the sun's most dazzling center—p. 93). This metaphor alludes to the popular belief that looking directly into the sun can cause madness, a sort of divine madness. The image serves to render the transcendent quality of Usnelli's experience, the fragile nature of such wonder. "E nel cuore di questo sole era silenzio. Tutto quello che era lì in quel momento non poteva essere tradotto in nient'altro, forse nemmeno un ricordo" (And in the heart of this sun was silence. All that was there in that moment could not be translated into anything else, maybe not even a memory—p. 93). Once again, the very indescribability of the experience bespeaks its importance: the experience cannot be put into words, for words will not do it justice. In fact, as in "La spirale" and in the adventures of the *impiegato* and the *viaggiatore*, the experience, the powerful "sconvolgente" experience, is fleeting and may not endure even in memory.

Twenty-five years later, in 1983, Calvino was, in a James lecture at New York University entitled "The Written and the Unwritten Word," to echo these words as he struggled with the relationship between the world and language:

> Now I have only . . . to test that the world outside is still there, and doesn't depend on words, is to some extent irreducible to words, and no speech, no writing could exhaust it. I have just to turn my back on the words deposited in books, dive into the outside world, and I will join *the heart of silence, the very silence full of meaning . . .* How can I reach it?[43] [Italics mine]

Yet, distinguishing the poet-alter ego from Calvino in "L'avventura di un poeta," we can say that Calvino has in fact translated some of that experience into words, and transmitted that wonder, as well as the lover's sense of frustration in sharing the writer's battle with language.

5

Preserving the Self and
Tearing the Other to Pieces

The threat of the Other: A negative erotic dimension

To this point, this study has devoted itself to the exploration of the erotic as a very positive dimension of human experience in Calvino's ideology. The erotic is fundamental to the development of identity and individuality, and takes at some points a cosmic form that links human erotic experience to all erotic expression and impulse through time. However, to explore only this dimension would be to leave half the story untold. At least one negative dimension to eros exists in Calvino's fiction, and he addresses it in part, as we will see, in a 1981 interview.[1] This final section will attend to the darker side of love, evident in many of Calvino's works.

The darker side of love appears contemporaneously with the "positive" view of love in "L'avventura di un poeta." While appreciating his relationship with Delia, Usnelli also feels that Delia is a threat to his relationship with the world around him. "Da quando amava Delia egli vedeva in pericolo il suo cauto, avaro rapporto con il mondo, ma non voleva rinunciare a nulla né di sé né della felicità che gli si apriva" (From the time he had come to love Delia, he saw his cautious, greedy relationship with the world endangered, but he didn't want to give any of it up, neither of himself nor of the happiness that opened up before him— Calvino, *Gli amori difficili*, p. 92). Delia is a very passionate creature who inspires in the poet, as we have seen, a certain wonder, a "sconvolgimento." His sense of self, that very ability to put thoughts into words of which his identity as a poet is comprised, is threatened.

While the erotic experience is essential, therefore, to the development of individual identity, it can at the same time constitute a threat to it. This other dilemma in Calvino's construct of eros can be thus articulated: on the one hand, the plenitude and strength of the individual, the tension to be oneself as much as possible, forms—as we have seen—a necessary foundation for desire; on the other hand, this thrust toward the Other, toward Otherness, may result in a threat to the self, because love involves a loss of self, a "sconvolgimento" and a loss of control. To say it another way: while love is characterized by a desire for complete union, for a total loss of self, it is also essential in Calvino's eyes to retain one's individuality and identity. Calvino, in his 1981 interview, states that a love relationship is most successful when the lovers are fully themselves, resisting both the natural inclination to overwhelm the Other and to be overwhelmed. An extremely delicate balance must be achieved.

We see seeds of this idea in the previously mentioned article by Spinazzola, who however separates male and female protagonists in his assessment of eros in Calvino. Speaking generally about Calvino's male characters, he says:

> Per l'altro verso però la femminilità lo impaurisce e respinge, facendogli pervenire la richiesta minacciosa d'una rinuncia al godimento intero della propria autonomia. L'acquisto gli pare allora convertirsi in perdita, giacché la soddisfazione del desiderio erotico esige un prezzo irreparabile di spossessamento vitale.[2]

> On the other hand however femininity frightens and repulses him, bringing to him the threatening demand of a renouncing of the complete enjoyment of his own autonomy. The gain then seems to him to become a loss, since the satisfaction of the erotic desire requires the unavoidable price of a vital dispossession.

In the 1981 interview for radio and television, in which quite a few prominent Italian authors were asked to consider issues on life in the next millennium, Calvino briefly addresses problems of old age, the division of domestic roles, and love—specifically, love as a threat.[3] However, Calvino makes no distinction between men and women as victims of the "overwhelming" effect of love and the Other. This particular interview appears to be little known, or at least little considered, by his critics. Some of Calvino's opinions on love are particularly pertinent and illuminating for our discussion.

When asked, "What will become of love in the year 2000?" Calvino offers, as he does in many of his answers, more advice than prediction, more counsel than soothsaying. He asserts,

"L'amore ha degli aspetti che sono costanti e degli aspetti che cambiano secondo le epoche" (Love has aspects that are constant and aspects that change according to the times—Finocchiaro-Chimirri, *Italo Calvino*, p. 93). He then acknowledges that, although possessiveness may be an unavoidable component of love, "mi pare auspicabile che sia eliminata nelle forme che sono state praticate fino a oggi, che sia vissuta in altro modo" (It seems advisable to me that it be eliminated in the forms in which it has been practiced up till now, that it be lived in another way—p. 93). His next words resonate with a cynically humorous awareness of love as a dark and unavoidably theatening force, but offer as well a sort of antidote:

> L'istinto di sopraffazione dell'altro in qualche misura è sempre presente nell'amore: ma sarebbe bene che s'instaurasse almeno un ritmo d'alternanza nella sopraffazione dell'altro, un piacere di comportarsi a parità di forze nello sbranarsi a vicenda. (P. 93)

> The instinct to overwhelm the Other is in some measure always present in love: but it would be well to establish at least an alternating rhythm in the overwhelming of the Other, a pleasure in the wielding of equal strength in the reciprocal tearing of the Other to pieces.

He answers along the same lines when questioned about jealousy. He admits that perhaps a certain amount is integral to the way we as humans experience love, but points out that it is more destructive to the one who suffers the jealousy than to the object of the jealousy. He suggests, "Quello che può cambiare è il modo di viverla, per riuscire a essere se stessi, pienamente se stessi, nel rapporto amoroso" (What can change is the way in which it is lived, in order to be yourselves, fully yourselves, in the love relation—p. 94). He says that the disintegration of the rigid male-female roles may be the first step, without, however, the sacrifice of the differences between the two.[4]

In response to whether an equality of the sexes is possible in love relationships, Calvino replies that perhaps it has, in some successful cases, already occurred. However, he reiterates his ideal of difference, although he seems to veer away from male-female difference—as we can see by his subsequent avoidance of genderizing terms—to focus on personality differences, and states that "equality" does not mean "uniformity": "L'amore è un rapporto tra diversi, tra individualità, ci deve essere questa curiosità e questo piacere di essere insieme con una persona che è diversa da te" (Love is a relationship between different people, between individuals; there must be the curiosity and the pleasure of being with a person who is different from you—p. 94).

With these comments, Calvino reveals the complexity of his notions on love, to some extent evinced by our analysis. It seems that to love well is a very delicate prospect indeed in Calvino's eyes, if not distinctly paradoxical. On the one hand, it is implicit that the love relationship offers a challenge to the individual, a sort of test of individuality, a test of one's sense of self. The test is to be able to maintain this sense of self without being overwhelmed by the Other. On the other hand, Calvino perceives love as overwhelming; "sopraffazione" is inevitable, and all we can ask for is that the two players in the game of love are opponents equal to each other, i.e., worthy of each other. This proclivity toward "sopraffazione," expressed in a figurative tearing of the Other to pieces, appears very early on in Calvino's fiction in juxtaposition to a protagonist's attempts to strengthen and preserve his or her individuality. While at some points positive, this is also the negative aspect of love. A rather fierce, aggressive, violent side to eros surfaces. Perhaps the struggle between lovers, kindled by the internal conflict between self-preservation and the tendency to tear the Other apart, finds its best exemplification in Cosimo, hero of *Il barone rampante*, and in the short story "Sotto il sole giaguaro" from the eponymous unfinished collection. However, other texts also reveal this dark, pessimistic conviction that in human interaction—and especially within the intimacy of erotic encounter—a certain "sbranarsi a vicenda" is inevitable.

Perhaps the very first time Calvino uses the infinitive "sbranarsi" to characterize human interaction is in *Il visconte dimezzato*. The "bad" Medardo, when asked why he goes around tearing things to pieces ("straziare" is the verb Pamela uses—Calvino, *Il visconte dimezzato*, p. 55), responds that everyone does evil things, but at least he—unlike others—is aware of the evil consequences of his actions. Undoubtedly, the "good" Medardo is far less self-aware and so in a sense far more dangerous. The "bad" Medardo explains that because "ogni incontro di due esseri al mondo è uno sbranarsi" (every encounter between two beings on earth is a tearing of the Other to pieces), they have no other language except that of things torn to pieces to talk with each other (p. 55–56). Calvino has rather brilliantly chosen to portray this "sbranarsi" in literal terms, although Medardo—executor of the physical rending—is obviously alluding primarily to the intangible, emotional damage humans wreak upon each other. (One of the delightful aspects of Calvino's use of fantasy is the unexpected trade between literal and figurative meanings.) In this way, the "bad" Medardo communicates with everyone including Pamela, so that the "sbranarsi" rather paradoxically typifies the behavior of those who "love" as well.

In *Il barone rampante*, set in the revolutionary period in Italy, Calvino creates perhaps the strongest literary exemplification of his ideas on the struggle for individuality against domination. Cosimo struggles not to be overwhelmed by Violante.[5] Cosimo Piovasco, protagonist of Calvino's classic, has been construed by many critics (to a greater or lesser degree) as a positive and exemplary figure, although some critics have identified him as a regressive character.[6] This young aristocrat, at the age of twelve, in a fit of defiance which eventually signals the beginning of his growth as an individual and of his self-determination, breaks free of paternal rule and climbs a tree. Unexpectedly, he decides never to descend again, and this spontaneous act becomes what Calvino himself, in the guise of Tonio Cavilla (an anagram for Calvino's name), claims in his introduction to the 1965 middle school edition is the first lesson of the novel: "La prima lezione che potremmo trarre dal libro è che la disobbedienza acquista un senso solo quando diventa una disciplina morale più rigorosa e ardua di quella a cui si ribella" (The first lesson we can draw from the book is that disobedience only makes sense when it becomes a moral discipline more rigorous and arduous than the one you are rebelling against).[7] The word "moral" sounds a by now familiar note to the reader. Yet, as J. R. Woodhouse points out, Calvino's approach is "undogmatic," and Calvino "declares that his readers may find in them [his creations] what they wish."[8]

Within the context of this fantastical novel, however, if we accept Cosimo as an exemplary figure, then the rigorous moral may refer to Cosimo's fierce determination to remain in the trees while at the same time contributing to, and participating in, the society around him. His moral may be his adherence to his sense of identity and his personal code of ethics. Cosimo's identity consists of his maintaining his position in the trees while remaining active in human affairs. He is "a solitary who did not avoid people."[9]

A brief study of a technique for characterization in *Il barone rampante* that becomes also a method for thematic development will prove that Cosimo is in essence meant to provide a paradigm for moral social and individual behavior. Hardly any critic has analyzed this popular novel through this technique, although one might suggest that the 1960 introduction and the notes to the 1965 edition hint at this narrative structure. In the preface to the 1960 edition of *I nostri antenati*, Calvino tells us about the characters: "Il dato che li accomuna quasi tutti è di essere solitari, ognuno con una maniera sbagliata d'esserlo, intorno a quell'unica maniera giusta che è quella del protagonista" (What almost all of them have in common is that they are solitaries, each in a wrong way, surrounding that single correct way that is the protagonist's—p. xvii). In the 1965 note to the much-discussed Gian de' Brughi chapter, Cavilla suggests, "Il contrasto tra l'ex-brigante che rimbecillisce a leggere romanzi e Cosimo che attraverso la lettura diventa uomo responsabile e attivo, può rappresentare lettura come evasione e lettura come formazione" (The contrast between the ex-brigand who grows stupid by reading novels and Cosimo who through his reading becomes an active and responsible man can represent literature as escape and literature as formation).[10] These comments point to a narrative structure which involves the development of the characterization technique of likeness and contrast. That is, almost every character that Cosimo encounters has something superficially in common with him, but is essentially his opposite. In fact, almost every encounter between Cosimo and another character or group of characters serves to sharpen Cosimo's identity, and specifically his strengths as contrasted to these characters' weaknesses. S. M. Adler also divines this narrative structure in *Il barone rampante* and points to a revealing comment by Calvino in a letter to Mario Boselli: "Anche per questa struttura potrai trovare una serie di riferimenti in altre narrazioni mie che sono costruite così: con al centro una relazione ax data come esemplare, e intorno una raggera o casistica di relazioni bx, cx, dx, etc." (Even for this structure you can find a series of references in my other narratives that are constructed like this: with at the center the relation *ax* given as exemplary and around it a circle of rays, or possibilities, of the relationships *bx*, *cx*, *dx*, etc.).[11]

Without digressing into an explication of this theory, we would like to suggest that Cosimo's relation to Violante is organized around this structure, as is Cosimo's eventual momentary betrayal of his sense of self in the chapters depicting his Orlandian madness.

Violante spells temptation from the very first moment Cosimo sets eyes on her in the Ondariva garden, previously out of bounds to him. Furnished with apple and trees, the garden very much resembles a child's version of Eden.[12] She is the very first character who tries to cajole and trick him out of the trees by trying to get him to the ground to push her swing and then, finally, by overturning the seat of the swing on which Cosimo stands. From the first instance, therefore, she presents a threat to his sense of self, and tries to make him violate the rules and self-defining boundaries he has only just set for himself.

Ironically, both Violante and Cosimo share one very strong priority: the uncompromising desire for liberty, a very strong Revolutionary and Enlightenment principle. In this way, they appear similar. However, their encounters indicate that the similarity is only superficial, and that their different definitions of liberty form the basis for all their future conflicts and for the very different courses of their lives. Cosimo believes in a universal liberty, and his own sense of personal liberty does not trespass on that of his neighbor. Violante's idea of liberty is selfish and depends on the subordination of others to her needs; as a *femme fatale*, she pursues only her own freedom, at others' expense. Her behavior in the garden indicates as much.

Their perceptions of love are also antithetical and represent two classic views of love: Violante feels that "l'amore è tutto"[13] while for Cosimo, who would like to love "rationally," love is one of life's many activities, like "la potatura" (pruning—Calvino, *Il barone rampante*, p. 186). Our representative of the Enlightenment claims: "Ogni cosa, a farla ragionando, aumenta il suo potere" (Each thing, when done through reason, increases its power—p. 193). Ironically, Cosimo is not able to understand Viola's games. The phrase, "non capire," referring to Cosimo's lack of understanding, appears at least three times in the description of one of their arguments (pp. 186–87) and then again several times at the end of their affair (p. 203).

Cosimo realizes in the end that he has lost her because he has not understood her. In fact, throughout their love affair, the "rational" Cosimo's actions are emotionally motivated: he is consumed by jealousy. Cosimo seems to be an example of Calvino's observation in the 1981 interview that jealousy is more harmful to the one who is jealous rather than the object of jealousy. In fact, Cosimo is far removed from the clear-sighted, active intellectual of the previous chapters. He has lost his sense of self. His fury against his rivals, his distress, his jealousy belie his very words on rationality and love. He has lost control. He is the opposite of what he was and does the opposite of what he says he believes. Reason and love seem to be incompatible, Calvino seems to be saying. Cosimo's downfall results from a loss of perspective, a loss of that critical distance which "living in the trees" symbolizes,[14] so necessary to understanding things and yet so difficult to maintain when one is in love. Their conflict can be thus summarized: Violante feels that love should be "rinuncia di sé" while Cosimo upholds that "non ci può essere amore se non si è se stessi con tutte le proprie forze" (love cannot exist if we are not ourselves with all our might—p. 201).

This last comment clearly indicates that Calvino's view of love, as expounded in the aforementioned 1981 interview, clearly supports Cosimo's philosophy over Violante's. However, there are several ironies at play here. First, it appears to be Violante who manages to stay clear-headed and manipulate the situation, while Cosimo loses his ability to think. Second, Cosimo, in a sense, is refusing to accept Violante for what she is, in his insistence on his own ideas. However, she does succeed in overwhelming him, in the "sopraffazione" that Calvino cautioned against in his 1981 interview.

After their relationship disintegrates, Cosimo goes "mad," like the furious Orlando of one of Calvino's favorite authors, Ariosto, and finally becomes the antithesis of what he had earlier believed in. Up to this point in the novel, the likeness-contrast characterization method which is the basis of this novel's narrative structure had functioned as a sort of process of elimination to formulate an ideal embodied in Cosimo. Cosimo's choices in life-style and attitude were shown to be superior to the other characters'. However, at this point, the technique undercuts Cosimo's status as hero and paradigm temporarily to focus instead on ideal behavior, so that the novel seems to concentrate not so much on the creation of a fairy-tale hero, an infallible legendary figure, but on an exemplary way of life, difficult to depict except through contrast.

The "mad" Cosimo in chapter 24 resembles ostensibly the earlier Cosimo the village people termed "mad." Cosimo uses the same tools: his writing, his speeches, and his rational abilities. He is still eccentric, but how does this new eccentricity differ from the other? Before, Cosimo was a nonconformist motivated by intellectual and human interests. He lived a life of "rigorous moral discipline." Now, emotional impulse rules him and his behavior appears simply as an outlet, as a wild expression. Before, he was socially conscious and committed; now, he's self-absorbed. Before, he wrote pamphlets on social reform; now, he writes them on the rights of woodpeckers.

Of course, Cosimo eventually snaps out of this frenzy, this furor, and gathers his wits, thanks to a social crisis which demands his attention. However, the madness episode reveals the extent to which love caused him to lose himself, despite his proclamation that maintaining one's individuality is the best way to love. Once again, love and individuality seem to be at odds with each other. We recall Medardo's words, "ogni incontro di due esseri al mondo è uno sbranarsi." While Medardo has made these figurative words literal, the baron's love affair with Violante exposes the emotional rending to pieces of the Other. In a sense, Violante "violates" the boundaries of Cosimo's individuality.

In *Il castello*, Calvino draws us into a Tarot world of medieval protagonists, of superstition, apocalypse, prophecy and primitive forces. This world, replete with supernatural beings and fantastical and eschatological happenings, offers several instances of a sort of "sbranare," of a tearing to pieces. For example, the ungrateful lover is required to strip himself of his identity, to drown himself in the forest, to allow himself to become dismembered. The followers of Cybele cut him to pieces, in fact. There are many instances of the violent world lovers inhabit. One scene particularly pertinent to our study is the story of the vampires, which includes the gruesome description of a wife who has killed her husband and who returns during the solstices as a witch and "lo disterra, gli ridà vita nutrendolo delle proprie vene" (she unearths him, she gives him life nourishing him with her own veins).[15] This particular detail introduces the theme of cannibalism, albeit with mitigated impact, as it is merely one more gruesome detail in a fictional world regulated by gruesome rules. Cannibalism might be seen as an ulterior step in the themata of "sbranarsi a vicenda"—a rending of limb from limb is followed by consumption of the parts. This theme of violence is more fully developed in a very different setting in the story "Sotto il sole giaguaro," the analysis of which will close this study. However, before embarking on this analysis, which will disclose the linguistic, thematic and ideological interworkings of the points we have so far undertaken, it may be useful to briefly mention a form of love that underlies many of Calvino's texts in varying shapes and functions, and which has been perhaps explored by critics primarily in relation to *Le cosmicomiche*. Cosmic love, a complex, many-sided force in Calvino's writings, appears in different forms and embraces texts from *Il barone rampante* (1957) to *Sotto il sole giaguaro* to *Palomar* (1983).

Cosmic love: Other forms

Studies on cosmic love have often limited themselves to *Le cosmicomiche*, in which the protean Qfwfq, the unchanging protagonist in changing forms ranging from cell to human male, has anthropomorphized the love between nonhuman beings to reveal eros as the force behind creation as well as procreation. Love is cosmic in this context insofar as it is a force experienced at all evolutionary stages and unites all animal life forms. It is also the catalyst for the development of the cosmos, as we see in "Tutto in un punto" or in "La spirale." Desire is the force that promotes development. It is not a morbid, negative emotion, a decadent emotion, but a natural force, at the heart of humanity's most instinctive behavior and needs. Calvino himself underlines the centrality of desire as a cosmic force in his study on Northrop Frye's well-known book *An Anatomy of Criticism*. It is worth reproducing the significant preface to his article, in which Calvino quotes the exerpt from Frye's classic that proved significant for him:

> Civilization is not merely an imitation of nature, but the process of making a total human form out of nature, and it is impelled by the force that we have just called desire. The desire for food and shelter is not content with roots and caves: it produces the human forms of nature that we call farming and architecture. Desire is thus not a simple response to need, for an animal may need food without planting a garden to get it, nor is it a simple response to want, or desire *for* something in particular. It is neither limited to nor satisfied by objects, but is the energy that leads human society to develop its own form.[16]

The scope of Calvino's own vision of eros seems to be reflected in Frye's words. The next half of the excerpt underlines the connection between creation, art and desire:

> Desire in this sense is the social aspect of what we met on the literal level as emotion, an impulse toward expression which would have remained amorphous if the poem had not liberated it by providing the form of its expression. The form of desire, similarly, is liberated and made apparent by civilization. The efficient cause of civilization

is work, and poetry in its social aspect has the function of expressing, as a verbal hypothesis, a vision of the goal of work and the forms of desire.[17]

This view succeeds on the one hand in demystifying "human" love while on the other hand it raises the erotic force to enormous heights. *Le cosmicomiche* does not provide the only proof that Calvino perceives eros as all-encompassing, a force that links humans today to their animal ancestors, and provides a basis for continuity along the evolutionary ladder. For example, we glimpse this cosmic vision of love already in Cosimo, whose communion with nature has been noted by such scholars as Woodhouse and Olken. Cosimo, who learns a great deal from living in the trees by observing the natural world around him, gets some of his first lessons—like many who live close to Nature—on sex from the animals as well as people. Love to Cosimo in his youth is a mystery, an untried experience, that fills him with wonder and envy when he sees couples meeting behind bushes in the night. He has begun to "sognare d'amore" (dream of love—Calvino, *Il barone rampante*, p. 143). However, embarrassed to indulge in voyeurism, he turns to the animal world vibrant with the energies of spring. The world of love that opens to him is an idyllic vision, in which the erotic state is a condition natural to all creatures and one that anthropomorphizes the natural world, almost romanticizing it:

> A primavera il mondo sopra gli alberi era un mondo nuziale: gli scoiattoli s'amavano con mosse e squittii *quasi umani*, gli uccelli s'accoppiavano sbattendo le ali, anche le lucertole correvano via unite, con le code strette a nodo; e i porcospini parevano diventati morbidi per rendere più dolci i loro abbracci. (P. 143, italics mine)

> In the spring the world in the trees was a nuptial world: the squirrels loved each other with *almost human* movements and squeals, birds coupled by flapping their wings, even the lizards ran away together, joined by their tails; and the porcupines seemed to become soft in order to make their embraces sweeter. (Italics mine)

In *Il barone rampante*, human love is not quite so simple or positive. When Cosimo finally sees Violante again after her long absence, his ability to communicate with her, to get her attention, is impeded by overwhelming emotion which causes animal sounds, bird noises, to issue from his throat. This behavior reveals the intensity of Cosimo's emotion, his loss of control, as well as the primitiveness of his feelings. The colorful images also serve to render Cosimo's overwhelming emotion; he imitates "il verso della beccaccia"; "un verso lungo e triste come quello del piviere"; "il tubare dell'upupa"; "il trillo della pispola"; and "il fitto cinguettio degli uccelli del giardino" (the cry of the woodcock; a long, sad cry like that of the plover—p. 176; the cooing of the hoopoe; the trill of the titlark; the dense chirping of the birds in the garden—p. 177). Calvino's apparent preference for Cosimo's insistence on an "amore naturale" (p. 184) over Violante's more refined and sophisticated games further underscores his vision of a cosmic, natural type of love.[18] A parallel exists between the force that drives Cosimo and the animals, as had been suggested by the anthropomorphizing of the animals' relations. This is yet another form of cosmic love in Calvino's work.

The erotic force thus levels the differences between human and animal urges and grounds both in primal, creative instinct. Perhaps one of the best illustrations of this—and of yet another form of cosmic love—is a short story from *Sotto il sole giaguaro*, called "Il nome, il naso," which explores the sense of smell. It was originally published in English in *Antaeus* (1976).[19] This story explores the importance of olfaction on the lives of three protagonists—a man who moves in aristocratic circles, a prehistoric man, and a struggling rock musician—whose stories are narrated in interwoven segments. Smell is central to their lives and to the pursuit of the feminine, who seems to embody their ideal and symbolize the *eterno femminino*, but is also as individual, as specific for them, as the female mollusk to Qfwfq. The Parisian pursues a woman through his memory of her perfume, while the other two pursue the feminine through her particular body odor. They are unable to locate these female protagonists, however, and all three eventually lose them to Death. The erotic drive experienced and pursued through the sense of smell unites the vastly different protagonists. The prehistoric man's urge does not appear any less valid or any more disreputable than that of the other two. In fact, we might say that the gloomiest, most squalid description is that of the asphyxiating, oppressive atmosphere of the musician's hotel room. That is perhaps the most "dehumanizing" of the three experiences. The prehistoric man, straddling both the human and animal rungs of the evolutionary ladder, represents another image of cosmic love. The human erotic urge is grounded in nature and likened to animal impulse, but not debased.

Primitive, "animalistic" urges in Calvino do not therefore appear to debase, but seem rather to illuminate and revitalize human eros. *Palomar*, a complex and provocative exercise in the art of description, offers yet another illustration of cosmic love.[20] In the chapter "Gli amori delle tartarughe," a certain anthropomorphization occurs through Palomar's observations. The title itself, by its use of the word "amori," introduces a human perspective. Also, the foreplay, the turtles' game of pursuit, provides for Palomar parallels between human and turtle eros, and grounds for reflection. However, Palomar cannot intuit, and therefore imagine or anthropomorphize, the turtles' sensations. This leads him to inquire into the nature of eros, to explore its identity as a mechanism:

> But what we call eros—is it perhaps only a program of our corporeal bodies, more complicated because the memory receives messages from every cell of the skin, from every molecule of our tissues, and multiplies them and combines them with the impulses transmitted by our eyesight and those aroused by the imaginations? The difference lies only in the number of circuits involved: from our receptors billions of wires extend, linked with the computer of feelings, conditionings, the ties between one person and another.[21]

This view of eros as mechanism, an interweaving of mental and physical messages, recalls "Priscilla." One would expect that such a view would demystify eros, banalize it. Yet Palomar wonders what the erotic might be like if there were a shell instead of the skin which is such an important part of the human erotic experience ("skin touched, seen, remembered"—p. 23). He also speculates on the components and functions of the erotic which seem to liberate it from a simply mechanistic identity. Strangely, his speculations lead him to inquire whether the turtle's eros might not actually be superior to ours, a very clear indication that the erotic in the animal world can be enlightening, and that it is certainly not considered by Calvino to be an "inferior" form of eros. Palomar wonders:

> The poverty of their sensorial stimuli perhaps drives them to a concentrated, intense mental life, leads them to a crystalline inner awareness . . . Perhaps the eros of tortoises obeys absolute spiritual laws, whereas we are prisoners of a machinery whose functioning remains unknown to us, prone to clogging up, stalling, exploding in uncontrolled automatisms. (Calvino, *Mr. Palomar*, p. 21)

The vision we are given here is one of eros as a profound, vital force, cosmic in its nature.

Further investigation into the roots of cosmic love brings us back to Calvino's comment in the 1961 article on cosmic love in the fiction of Jorge Luis Borges (it is also quoted in his less extremist 1969 article in a footnote). While acknowledging his earlier radical position, Calvino uses his excerpt from the earlier article to confirm his conviction that eros can only be portrayed indirectly, which is one of the points common to the two articles, one of the points of continuity in his opinion. He thus praises the great Argentine writer:

> Jorge Luis Borges ha espresso il trasporto amoroso in racconti dove un'immagine di donna si collega a un simbolo di totalità cosmica (vedi *Lo Zahir* e *L'Aleph*) raggiungendo per via intellettuale una dimensione emotiva che per la solita via della mimesi decadentistica delle sensazioni non ci si sognerebbe neanche.[22]

> Jorge Luis Borges expressed erotic transport in stories where the image of the woman is linked to a symbol of cosmic totality (see *El Zahir* and *El Aleph*), thus reaching by intellectual means an emotional dimension that we would not even be able to imagine through the usual route of the decadent mimesis of sensation.

We recall that at the end of that article Calvino proposes to "stabilire una comunicazione erotica con i materiali e gli oggetti della nostra più squallida vita quotidiana," "immaginando rapporti sessuali non antropomorfi (come ho tentato io, raccontando amori di molluschi o di organismi unicellulari)" (establish an erotic communication with the materials and objects of our most squalid everyday life [. . .] by imagining nonanthropomorphic sexual relationships, as I have tried to do by recounting the loves of mollusks or unicellular organisms).[23] These statements indicate that restoring the erotic element to everyday life by presenting it in unexpected and positive ways might be part of his "moral option." Cosmic love, in this scale of values, certainly has a high place.[24] Keeping in mind both Calvino's vision of an encompassing cosmic love, necessary to all creation, as well as his awareness of the darker, threatening side of love, we can proceed to our final analysis, in which thematic and linguistic theories merge.

"Sotto il sole giaguaro": A merging of linguistic and erotic theories

Perhaps the most appropriate beginning to our analysis of "Sotto il sole giaguaro" might be to glance at an episode of *Palomar* with which it shares a common setting, symbols, and perhaps a character as well: "Serpenti e teschi." These two stories about voyages to Mexico were published for the first time in the same year, 1983 (the former, according to the bibliographic information in the 1986 translation into English, first appeared in the New Yorker in 1983). The stories effect a thematic counterpoint to each other, and present two approaches to knowledge, to both of which Calvino seems sympathetic.[25] The two narratives offer, through a voyage to Mexico that is also a voyage in hermeneutics—for the protagonist explores some of the ancient ruins and symbols he finds—different attitudes which characterize two contrasting, complementary strains in Calvino's thoughts.

In Palomar, the section entitled "Serpenti e teschi" might evoke, according to current semiotic codes, expectations of a discussion of death (the skull), sin or evil or continuity (the serpent), or possibly some Christian interpretation in the juxtaposition of such symbols. However, the story thwarts such expectations and focuses instead on the conflicting positions of two characters: 1) the friend (Salustiano in "Sotto il sole giaguaro?") who guides Palomar through the ruins recounting legends from pre-Columbian cultures and transforming every stone bass relief (significantly, the jaguar figures amongst the animals mentioned in the bass reliefs) "into a cosmic tale, an allegory, a moral reflection" (p. 96); and 2) his antithesis, a young teacher who has brought his class to view the ruins of the civilization and who simply gives the historical and technical data ("the teacher tells what civilization they belong to, what century, what stone they are carved from"—p. 98) and refuses to hazard an interpretation of the symbols, as we see in his flat reaffirmation, "We don't know what they mean" (p. 96). Nor does his assessment waver of a figure that is central as well to the other short story, the statue of a "chac-mool," despite the fact that experts have unanimously agreed on its meaning, as we read in Palomar.

Palomar—like Calvino—is attracted to both his friend's passion for interpretation as well as the young teacher's refusal to interpret, which had initially struck him as indifference. In fact, given that the details of the contexts in which these prehistoric figures were drawn are lost to modernity, the teacher's methodical refusal to impose modern hermeneutics on these figures and to take them rather on the simplest literal level seems to Palomar "perhaps the only way to evince respect for their secret; trying to guess is a presumption, a betrayal of that true, lost meaning" (p. 97).

Calvino, in his 1984 interview with Lucente, discusses these two approaches to hermeneutics:

> These are two different attitudes, and I recognize the force of each of them. We cannot do without interpreting, without asking ourselves what something means, without embarking on an explanation. At the same time, however, we know that for any explanation . . . too many things are missing, because we lack the entire context. Even if we succeed in establishing certain meanings with precision, these so-called meanings, in our context, are entirely different.[26]

The two Mexicans finally clash over the interpretation of the figure of the serpent with the skull in its fangs. Addressing the young teacher, the students and Palomar, the friend interprets it as the continuity between life and death, as an affirmation of the cycle of life, but the teacher corrects him as he and his class move away. Although Calvino claims in his interview with Lucente that he limits himself to presenting the two approaches rather than choosing one,[27] Palomar's final thoughts amount to a choice that paves the way for the other version of the Mexican voyage in "Sotto il sole giaguaro" and thus seems an aesthetic choice on the part of the author. Palomar appears to select the friend's perspective:

> he knows he could never suppress in himself the need to translate, to move from one language to another, from concrete figures to abstract words, to weave and reweave a network of analogies. Not to interpret is impossible, as refraining from thinking is impossible. (Calvino, Mr. Palomar, p. 100)

These comments serve as a perfect opening for "Sotto il sole giaguaro," a story which is precisely that attempt to translate these same Mexican figures into a coherent cosmic story, and thereby offer new meanings to contemporary society. Perhaps these two versions of the same theme best reflect Calvino's skepticism and optimism, his reluctance to assign definite meaning and his inability not to, his diffidence in assigning a relation between symbol and significance, object and language, and his affirmation of this relation.

The motif of "translation" mentioned in *Palomar* also functions in different ways in the other account of the tour of Mexico that is "Sotto il sole giaguaro." The first line of the story, "Oaxaca si pronuncia Uahàca" makes a translation from one code of pronunciation to another.[28] The sound of the name of the city also immediately sets the scene in Mexico, while giving a sense as well that a pre-Columbian context will be translated into a European language. The idea of translation assumes broad impact in its use as cultural translation, a translation of cultures over space and time.

The first paragraph introduces most of the thematic threads to be developed through the course of the narrative. The first sentence offers several possible interpretations, and underscores as well the importance of precision in language in its attempt to render most vividly and authentically a foreign word. The importance of precision in pronunciation can be seen in the English translation of this story which reads, "'Oaxaca' is pronounced 'Wahaka.'"[29] Calvino, as we have repeatedly seen, reiterated the centrality of his ideal of linguistic precision through the course of his career. To those earlier articles on "precision" in language and to Corti's interview can be added the conference he gave at the New York Institute for the Humanities in 1983, the same year he published *Palomar* and "Sotto il sole giaguaro" (the latter written in 1982). This conference appeared for the first time in Italian in 1985 as "Mondo scritto e mondo non scritto." In this article, in which he mentions both *Palomar* and "Sotto il sole giaguaro," he once again condemns specifically the continuing "abstraction" in the Italian language; he sees it as a "plague" which writers must fight by using a language that is "direct" and "concrete"[30]—that is, tending toward clarity, communication, and precision. The author's insistence on precision is also evinced in his detailed reproduction of recipes and in his attempt to reproduce vivid sensory experience in "Sotto il sole giaguaro." (In this same essay, Calvino says: "Another book I'm writing is about the five senses, in order to demonstrate that contemporary man has lost the use of them.")[31]

However, this beginning sentence and the ensuing descriptions of his travels also endeavor to instruct and inform the reader. Our Introduction addressed the great deal of speculation that has occurred over Calvino's belief in an "edifying" literature, which has become inextricably interwoven with postmodern concerns about literature's ability to reach outside itself. However, the abundance of detail that characterizes Calvino's fiction—e.g., the description of species of birds and trees in *Il barone rampante*, the types of perfumes named in "Il nome, il naso" and all the cultural and gastronomical details in the story of his journey to Mexico—might suggest that the author wishes to impart information. One might go so far as to say that *Sotto il sole giaguaro* seems to praise the power of language, to reassign it a power it has lost.

Not to be overlooked, in fact, is the importance of the names of things, like the name of the city, or the names of the foods, whose recipe Calvino often gives his reader. The name of the city serves to render more effectively the Mexican setting, as do the names of the foods. They try to render a very specific—nongeneric, undiluted—sense of the essence of Mexico for the narrator. Names—words—seem also, in this story, to have a certain magical, mystical, transformational power, as well. So this word "Oaxaca," with all its vowels and its fricative, seems to hint at some of the mystery to come.

Let us continue the in-depth analysis of this very suggestive and rich beginning paragraph. The next sentence tells us that the hotel used to be a convent, the convent of Santa Catalina. This next step in the creation of a setting also introduces the theme of a juxtaposition of two different moments in time: a religious past and a more secular present. The story constantly moves between past and present, so that the present is overlaid with the atmosphere of a mysterious and inexplicable past. In fact, entering this hotel seems to mean entering a past era that is somehow also contemporaneous, because it lives on in the disturbing picture which hangs in the bar of the hotel, a bar called *Las Novicias*. Already with this first paragraph, the reader realizes that he and the narrator have entered a sacred dimension, another plane. There is a certain amount of irony, of course, directed at this fusion of the religious and secular in the country, for the convent, which once had shut the world out, now serves as a hotel. However, beyond this irony, the sacred atmosphere seems to be very strong, especially in the description of the painting.

This same coexistence, this fusion, of religious and worldly values continues in the painting. The fact that the young nun and old priest stand side by side and that their hands almost touch immediately suggests some sort of physical bond that transcends, or perhaps enhances, their religious connection. This canvas introduces one of the dominant themes in this story and in the other two stories: a love relationship, a love story.[32] The primitiveness of the picture and the rigidity of the figures, we are told, are typical of the colonial period, and transmit "una sensazione conturbante, come uno spasimo di sofferenza contenuta" (a disturbing sensation, like a spasm of repressed suffering—Calvino, *Sotto il sole giaguaro*, p. 29). This description transmits a sense of disturbing emotional intensity and mystery. The adjective "colonial" evokes yet another motif: that of the layering of civilizations typical of Mexico (and of all history), the blending of cultures which occurs in colonization. Implicit in this, as we will see, is the idea of domination; the new civilization dominates the other. For example, the religious in this first paragraph underlies the secular. Yet the underlying civilization never quite disappears, but rather seems to take the new civilization into it, to absorb it by allowing itself to be absorbed. For, in this paragraph, and in much of the story, what dominates is not so much the modern secular world, the tourism, but the strong mystical atmosphere, the sense of sacredness, and the conviction of other civilizations that live on. All this is implicit in the mention of a "colonial" art and will be elaborated. In this first paragraph, Calvino has managed to present the thematic motifs, as well as historical and athropological concerns, that will unfold, while immediately immersing his reader in the setting. He has succeeded in creating a strong sense of setting almost instantly.

While the idea of cultural dominance inherent in colonization reflects the struggles between civilizations, the story also explores struggles within the human soul and psyche. A hint of the internal conflicts, or perhaps of the coexistence of conflicting forces, surfaces in the subsequent paragraph, which describes the writing on the bottom of the canvas that seeks to justify why the nun and chaplain were painted together. In this justification, the noun "amore" is repeated three times, followed each time by an explanatory parenthetical comment. This word, which carries the broadest implications and is exactly the kind of word that Calvino might say has lost meaning and impact through overuse and idealization, seems here to acquire *precision*. However, as we have seen, the experience of erotic love remains a challenge, in Calvino's writings, to the prowess of language, and often defies direct definition. Here, the "sacredness" of the erotic is intensified by the otherworldly "sacredness" of the characters.

The first parenthetical explanation is "La parola nella pia prosa spagnola si presentava carica del suo anelito ultraterreno" (The word in the pious Spanish prose was charged with its otherworldly yearning—pp. 29–30). It underscores the otherworldliness of the force of love that bound the two. The second reads: "la parola nella sua accezione spirituale sublimava ma non cancellava l'emozione corporea" (the word in its spiritual meaning sublimated but did not erase the corporeal emotion—p. 30). The adjectives "spirituale" and "corporea" signal the tension between antithetical psychological and ideological forces; the underlying physical impulse simmers beneath the spiritual one. This internal struggle further illustrates the motif of forces striving for dominance. The third parenthesis further explicates the intensity of the bond, thirty years strong, which caused the much younger abbess to expire upon the death of the chaplain: "la parola bruciava d'una verità in cui tutti i significati convergono" (the word burned with a truth in which all meanings converge—p. 30). Love comes to encompass all meanings and defies tepid, vague connotations. In fact, this might be considered another form of cosmic love, another way in which love embraces all aspects and dimensions of human living. The fact that the love the nun feels causes her to join him in heaven shows most clearly the coexistence of contradictory forces—and contradictory dogmas, for Catholic dogma dictates that the desire to go to heaven must be a desire to join God. Yet the secular and religious connotations of love here intermingle.

In the third paragraph we return to the present, and discover that Olivia has been *translating* the more difficult expressions (an autobiographical reference to Ester, Calvino's wife, who is a translator?).[33] Like the abbess and chaplain, Olivia and the narrator also have a long-standing relationship. Olivia's role as translator, however, functions not merely on a linguistic level, but on an emotional and sensorial level as well. Through her translation of sensory and other experience, her partner—the narrator—is better able to understand and appreciate these experiences. Many examples occur in the story. In the first, which occurs very early in the story, the narrator/protagonist admits that the series of thought associations which they share unravels in his mind "in modo più torpido e nebbioso, tale che senza di lei non . . . [avrebbe] potuto acquistarne coscienza" (in a fuzzier, more torpid manner, so that without her . . . I would not have been able to develop an awareness of it—pp. 30–31).[34] He needs her to become better aware of the world that surrounds him and of his own emotions; she is a sort of translator of life and sensory experience.

To return to the couple as they stand before the canvas: their reactions recall Calvino's 1969 article on sex and laughter. They are rendered speechless; words seem out of place, for it seems as if they are facing some intense drama, some "felicità." They are also strangely intimidated, frightened almost. We remember that the reaction of the poet in "L'avventura di un poeta," when confronted by happiness and love, was very similar. In the 1969 article, Calvino says that love is frightening, "sconvolgente." The intensity of the earthly and religious love transmits itself to the viewers; it conveys a sense of transcendent emotion, of sacredness. The narrator feels a consuming void and, like the poet, an inability to translate his feelings into words. He feels a certain loss of control, like that "sconvolgimento" mentioned in the article: "il senso di una mancanza, d'un vuoto divorante" (the sense of a lack, a devouring void—Calvino, *Sotto il sole giaguaro*, p. 30).

When the silent Olivia finally speaks, her words are so jarring, so pragmatic, that they snap the scene back into the present. Her "vorrei mangiare *chiles en nogada*" (I would like to eat *chiles en nogada*) is strikingly and humorously out of context. The association between the painting and her desire to eat *chiles en nogada* will be explained soon enough, but we recall that humor for Calvino is often a way to cope with intensity, especially the intensity of love (1969 essay on sex and laughter).

Olivia's hunger introduces the central theme of the story—the exploration of the sense of taste. The epigraph to the story (omitted in the English translation), which consists of an excerpt from N. Tommaseo's 1830 *Dizionario dei Sinonimi*, also suggests the theme:

Gustare, in genere, esercitare il senso del gusto, riceverne l'impressione, anco senza deliberato volere, o senza riflessione poi. L'assaggio si fa più determinante a fin di gustare e di sapere quel che si gusta; o almeno denota che dell'impressione provata abbiamo un sentimento riflesso, un'idea, un principio d'esperienza. (P. 27)

To taste, in general, to exercise the sense of taste, to receive an impression of it, even without deliberately wanting to, or without reflection. Tasting becomes more determinative the more one tastes and knows what is being tasted; or at least it denotes that we have a reflected sentiment, an idea, the beginning of an experience of the impression obtained.

From this epigraph, one might deduce that Calvino is interested in the sense of taste not only as a form of knowledge, but also as a sense that is heightened *by knowledge* of what is being tasted. (The original title of the short story was "Sapore, sapere.") Calvino seems to be suggesting that direct sensory experience, accompanied by an awareness of that experience, will intensify the sensory experience and expand one's knowledge of it; his message seems almost Galilean in its equation of sensory experience—personal observation—and knowledge. This may explain the role of the detailed recipes and the descriptions of degustation.

The rest of the epigraph supports this hypothesis by addressing the meaning of "sapere":

> Quindi è che *sapio*, ai Latini, valeva in traslato sentir rettamente; e quindi il senso dell'italiano *sapere*, che da sé vale dottrina retta, e il prevalere della sapienza sopra la scienza. (P. 29)

> Thus it is that *sapio* to the Latins figuratively meant to feel uprightly; and thus the meaning of the Italian *sapere*, that by itself means upright doctrine and the prevailing of knowledge over science.

A glance at what Tommaseo says under the heading "sapere" will illuminate the opposition he establishes between "sapienza" and "scienza": "La *scienza* conosce; la *sapienza* e conosce e contempla ed ama" (Science knows; knowledge knows and contemplates and loves).[35] Perhaps Calvino is implying that sensory experience will acquire meaning through knowledge, contemplation and love. (Not to be excluded is the possibility that the epigraph also plays on the other "impersonal" use of "sapere" in Italian: the intransitive verb refers to the ability to discern the taste [or smell] of something, e.g., "sapere di amaro" and "sapere di buono"—to taste bitter and to taste good.)

The theme of gustation achieves profound and dramatic proportions in this story. For example, the narrator makes direct reference to eating as a superior way of obtaining knowledge. Eating—taste—becomes a way to know the country he visits. Eating becomes both one of the ways the narrator travels, while constituting a voyage, a gastronomical journey, in and of itself:

> il vero viaggio, in quanto introiezione d'un "fuori" diverso dal nostro abituale, implica un cambiamento totale dell'alimentazione, un inghiottire il paese visitato . . . facendolo passare per le labbra e l'esofago. Questo è il solo modo di viaggiare che abbia un senso oggigiorno, quando tutto ciò che è visibile lo puoi vedere anche alla televisione senza muoverti dalla tua poltrona.[36] (P. 38–39)

> the real trip, in so far as it is an introjection of an "outside" that is different from our habitual one, implies a total change in food-intake, a swallowing of the country visited . . . having it pass through the lips and esophagus. This is the only way of traveling that makes sense today, when you can see everything that is visible on TV without budging from your armchair.

However, gustation far exceeds the boundaries of simple food consumption, and seems to embrace as a central theme, as we will see, all the minor themes. For example, mystical and earthly impulses join once again when we discover that the couple has been told that the nuns used to prepare the ancient recipes for the dishes they are currently enjoying. It is for this reason that Olivia, overcome by the intensity of the canvas, thinks of food. These two planes of human experience, physical and spiritual, which the nuns lived with extreme intensity, seem to meld and transform each other in the couple's awareness as they eat. This intensity is suggested by the description of "una cucina elaborata e audace, come tesa a far vibrare le note estreme dei sapori" (an elaborate and audacious cooking, as if straining to make the extreme notes of tastes vibrate—p. 31). The sensory experience permeates the imagination to such an extent, that, like the highest of mystical experiences, it involves all the senses: "una possessione assoluta esercitata sulla ricettività di tutti i sensi" (an absolute possession exercised over the receptivity of all the senses—p. 31).

Gustation is also important because, for the most part, the significant interactions between the narrator and Olivia occur at the dinner table, during meals in which they communicate through the sharing of foods. In fact, the narrator comments that their sex life has been for the most part suspended since their arrival in Mexico and that they have "per teatro non più il letto dei nostri abbracci ma una tavola apparecchiata" (no longer [their] bed of embraces as [their] theatre but a table that has been set—p. 37). One might say that their sexual impulses have been— as perhaps were those of the nuns—channeled through one sense, the sense of taste.

While the delicacies Olivia and the narrator share seem to have been the sole sensual enjoyment of the nuns, the spiciness and hotness and burning sensations also suggest a parallel. They work as a metaphor for their religious ecstasy. The narrator speaks of their "spinta verso l'estremo che portava all'esasperazione dei sapori amplificata dalla vampa dei *chiles* più piccanti" (drive toward the extreme that led to an exhaustion of flavors heightened by the fierce heat of the spiciest *chiles*—p. 33). The spiciness of their recipes expresses the intensity of their religious life. These recipes form a culinary *art*, which in its elaborate complexity seems to reflect a Baroque taste. These ideas are reflected in the narrator's speculations on the work of the nuns, most of whom were from noble families, and could leave to their servants the hard work of actually preparing the food:

> E quanto a loro non avevano che da ideare e predisporre e confrontare e correggere ricette che esprimessero le loro fantasie costrette tra quelle mura: fantasie anche di donne raffinate, e accese, e introverse, e complicate, donne con bisogni d'assoluto, con letture che parlavano d'estasi e trasfigurazioni e martirî e supplizi, donne con contrastanti richiami nel sangue, genealogie in cui la discendenza dei Conquistadores si mescolava con quella delle principesse indie, o delle schiave. (Pp. 32–33)

> And as for them, all they had to do was think up and plan and compare and correct recipes that expressed their fantasies hemmed in by those walls: the fantasies of women who were refined, and fiery, and introverted, and complicated, women with the need for absolutes, with readings that talked of ecstasies and trasfigurations and martyrdoms and torture, women with opposing callings in their blood, genealogies in which the descendants of the Conquistadors mixed with that of the Indian princesses, or with that of the women slaves.

The theme of dominance resurges in the Spanish noun, "conquistadores," in this passage; in the nuns, the blood of the invader and invaded mixes. A struggle for supremacy and dominance had already appeared in the form of the internal conflict between earthly and spiritual impulses, and was implicit in the colonization suggested by the colonial period portrait at the beginning. When the narrator mentions the Jesuits who came to Mexico to build a seminary, he presents another ideological conflict: the Christian versus the pre-Christian. The Jesuits had with their building tried to outdo their predecessors' constructions:

> Certo i Gesuiti s'erano proposti di gareggiare con lo splendore degli Aztechi, le rovine dei cui templi e palazzi . . . erano sempre presenti a ricordare un dominio esercitato con gli effetti suggestivi d'un'arte trasfiguratrice e grandiosa. (Pp. 33–34)

> Certainly the Jesuits had set out to compete with the splendor of the Aztecs, the ruins of whose temples and palaces . . . were always there as a reminder of a dominion exercised with the evocative effects of a grandiose and transfiguring art.

And, ever more directly addressing Mexico's identity as a stratification of cultures, as a country that has witnessed civilizations vying for dominance and ideas vying for supremacy:

C'era una sfida nell'aria . . . : l'antica sfida tra le civiltà d'America e di Spagna nell'arte d'incantare i sensi con seduzioni allucinanti, e dall'architettura *questa sfida s'estendeva alla cucina, dove le due civiltà s'erano fuse*, o forse dove quella dei vinti aveva trionfato, forte dei condimenti nati dal suo suolo. (P. 34, italics mine)

There was a challenge in the air . . . : the ancient challenge between American and Spanish civilizations in the art of bewitching the senses with dazzling sensations, and from architecture *this challenge extended to cooking, where the two civilizations had merged*, or maybe where that of the vanquished had triumphed, strong with the condiments sprung from its soil. (Italics mine)

Such a conflict, which the narrator seems to be in some way living through his gastronomic journeys, as well as through his trips to the ancient sites, adds to the sense of drama in the story. This capturing of historical, religious and spiritual conflict gives way to, and ultimately encompasses, the personal conflicts between Olivia and the narrator that exemplify the struggle for, and delicate balance of, power between lovers that Calvino had mentioned in his 1981 interview. The narrative thus moves back and forth between the individual and the universal, between macro- and micro-cosm, in order to establish a continuity between the two levels.

The visit to the Jesuit church is followed by an intimate dinner scene that refocuses on the description of local dishes and their taste, as well as on the couple's interaction through shared gustation. It is in this episode that the idea of dominance is introduced into the narrator's experience of his relationship. The narrator describes Olivia's varied and sensual enjoyment of the taste of the foods by describing the movement of her lips, evocative of an underlying erotic impulse sublimated and rechanneled. Olivia seems to communicate with him through their mutual appreciation of culinary delights. Her movements, her "carica vitale, certi suoi scatti o indugi o struggimenti o palpiti" (vital charge, certain of her jumpy movements or hesitations or longings or thrills) reach him without losing any of their intensity—at the table rather than in bed. In this way, having discovered yet another method for representing eros, the author manages to transmit their intimacy through a new vocabulary and a new setting for erotic love, while defying the "mimesi decadentistica" he had condemned long before.[37]

The couple is thus currently in the perfect state, observes the narrator, for understanding the love between the abbess and chaplain:

> Un amore che poteva pur essere stato, agli occhi del mondo e di loro stessi, perfettamente casto, e nello stesso tempo d'una carnalità senza limiti in quell'esperienza dei sapori raggiunta per mezzo d'una complicità segreta e sottile. (P. 37)

> A love that could have been, in the eyes of the world and in their own eyes, perfectly chaste, and at the same time of a boundless sensuality in that experience of flavors reached through a secret and subtle complicity.

The word "complicity" reassures the narrator that a certain equality ("parità," p. 38) does still exist between him and Olivia, whose obsession with food coupled with their lack of sex has left him feeling disoriented and insecure about their relationship and his place in it. (The noun, "parità," is the same used to advocate equality between partners by Calvino in his 1981 article.) The narrator has begun to feel like an observer, in a subordinate position, to her interest in food. However, the idea of complicity leads him to acknowledge the differences in how they experience and to appreciate these differences. However, his uncertainty, his fear of being dominated, is not resolved; it worsens throughout the story and finally reaches a crisis point.

With a shift back to the macrocosm, the theme of dominance shifts momentarily from the personal domain back to the historical to refocus on the struggle between civilizations, and specifically the ancient civilizations of Mexico, whose calendars indicate a belief that the universe ended every fifty-two years. The narrator posits the view that perhaps each new civilization was but the continuation of the old, evinced in the cycle of massacres represented in the bas-reliefs. The cyclic view of the cosmos, rejected—or at least questioned—in "Serpenti e teschi" in *Palomar*, here resurfaces. The destruction, the massacre, the bloody rites, are construed as an integral part of that primitive world. The disturbing, pessimistic implication is that such violence is at the very roots of civilization, is perhaps the very essence of human experience, a universal. In fact, Alonso the guide underscores the pivotal role violence assumes in the cycle of life in his explanatory pantomimes, which try to prove "che

un identico strazio chirurgico accomunava le nascite e le morti"
(that births and deaths shared a common surgical agony—p. 41).
In fact, each of the figures in the bas-reliefs seems somehow
linked to these bloody rites and rituals. This gory violence seems
to permeate all levels of experience. Violence is associated with
war, with the renewal of the universe, and even with the winner
of athletic games who becomes a sacrificial victim. Alonso, de-
scendant of one of those ancient civilizations, exclaims patrioti-
cally that it was an honor to be the victim of such a sacrifice.[38]
Alonso "si sentiva in dovere di esaltare l'offerta al sole d'un cuore
umano palpitante, perché l'aurora ritorni a illuminare il mondo
ogni mattina" (felt obligated to praise the sun offering of a palpi-
tating human heart, so that the dawn might return to light the
world every morning—p. 42). It is interesting to note that the
notions of a cyclic universe that Calvino explores in this short
story do not have biological roots, as in *Le cosmicomiche*, but
religious and historical roots. Those ancient peoples organized
their world according to religious beliefs.

The awareness of prevailing violence adds to the rising tension
in the narrator's archeological visits as well as in his interaction
with Olivia. Olivia, confronted by this glorification of bloody
rites, asks: What did they do with the victims' bodies? Uncomfortable, Alonso refuses to answer and leaves Olivia moody and
irritable. The question seems to bring the reader to the edge
of a precipice, in expectation of an unpleasant and unpalatable
revelation. At this point, the sense of violence, of struggle, has
permeated the narrator's perception of Olivia and, sitting opposite her on the jeep, he notices her teeth, immediately linking in
this way the motif of eating with the idea of violence. Suddenly,
jarringly, her teeth no longer bring to his mind her flashing smile;
instead, they appear as what they really are: tools for the purpose
of "l'affondare nella carne, lo sbranare, il recidere" (sinking into
flesh, tearing apart, tearing off—p. 43). We recall that "sbranare"
has referred to what *humans* do to each other in the fantastical
Il visconte dimezzato (both literally and figuratively), and in the
1981 interview the expression refers to the overwhelming and
destruction of the Other and the loss of self that can characterize
love relationships. Here, the verb apparently refers to food, but
given the preceding focus on violence, the narrator's insecurity,
and Olivia's suspect question, "sbranare" seems to vibrate with
menacing overtones.

The return to the hotel means a return to "civilization," to
the present, and another "scena conviviale"—a promotional tea

party for the upcoming presidential election offered to the wives of officials. At the tea party current rituals and formalities are offered in contrast to primitive ones, and new views of government and social order contrast with the ancients' theories on the structure of society. However, at this tea, the couple meets up again with their Mexican friend, Salustiano, and Olivia reiterates her disturbing question. Salustiano assumes his most confidential tone and satisfies Olivia by admitting that perhaps the victim, having become "cibo divino" (divine food), would be eaten. We recall that Calvino claimed one of literature's goals to be the rupture of taboos:

> The unconscious is the ocean of the unsayable, of what has been expelled from the land of language, removed as a result of ancient prohibitions. The unconscious speaks—in dreams, in verbal slips, in sudden associations—with borrowed words, stolen symbols, linguistic contraband, until literature redeems these territories and annexes them to the language of the waking world.[39]

Perhaps Salustiano's admission of cannibalism, one of the taboos of modern societies, can fall into this category of "territories to be redeemed by literature." The widespread implications of cannibalism begin to surface most explicitly, thanks to Olivia's continued curiosity and her insistence on bringing the issue further into the light. In fact, Salustiano's answer does not satisfy Olivia, who is—so to speak—"voracious," and demands more information about the preparation of the meal. Although one might have expected the mere mention of cannibalism to be off-putting, Olivia instead trespasses on taboos and refuses to be repulsed.

The association between food and cannibalism, and the suggestion of an existing, contemporary form of cannibalism, hovers on the fringes of the story. Thus in the middle of this discussion on the ritual meal, the narrator looks at Olivia's teeth and finds that her tongue and lips look prepared to devour.

In the subsequent dinner episode, another description of the menu is followed by a period of fantasizing on the part of the narrator. He imagines himself ingested by Olivia in a daring and illicit fusion of the motifs of food, cannibalism, dominance and the erotic. Calvino takes the common erotic metaphor of "eating" to its extreme:

> Era la sensazione dei suoi denti nella mia carne che stavo immaginando, e sentivo la sua lingua sollevarmi contro la volta del palato,

avvolgermi di saliva, poi spingermi sotto la punta dei canini . . . mi pareva che una parte di me, o tutto me stesso, fossi contenuto nella sua bocca, stritolato, dilaniato fibra a fibra. (Pp. 50–51)

It was the sensation of her teeth in my flesh that I was imagining, and I felt her tongue lift me against her palate, cover me in saliva, then push me under the tip of her canines . . . it seemed that a part of me, or all of me, was contained within her mouth, crushed, torn asunder fiber by fiber.

The "sbranare" has become literal in the imagination of the narrator, and has acquired an erotic charge. The narrator tells us, however, that his is not a passive role:

mentre venivo masticato da lei sentivo anche che agivo su di lei, le trasmettevo sensazioni che si propagavano dalle papille della bocca per tutto il suo corpo, che ogni vibrazione ero io a provocarla: era un rapporto reciproco e completo che ci coinvolgeva e travolgeva. (P. 51)

While I was being chewed by her I felt that I acted upon her too, that I transmitted sensations to her that spread from the papillae of her tongue to her entire body, that it was I who provoked every vibration: it was a complete and reciprocal rapport that involved and overcame us.

Once again, microcosm reflects macrocosm; the relationship absorbs and reflects the atmosphere of the Mexican journey. A circular movement of reciprocal enjoyment and destruction, of consumption, has been established between the partners, as had been established between warring civilizations. In addition, as in the fusion of warring cultures in the country's cuisine in which perhaps "quella dei vinti aveva trionfato," here too the "defeated," the "consumed"—the narrator—seems to exercise a certain power.

However, Olivia's dominant position in the relationship is reasserted by her discontent at her companion's silence, which incites her to resume a long-standing complaint about his "passivity." (This brings to mind Delia's discontent with the poet's silence and lack of verbal participation in her verbal transports.) The accusation "insipid" rings loudly in his ears, while the pun rings humorously in ours, and the narrator's sense of inadequacy increases.

The tension between the partners is resolved in the episode

surrounding the figure of the *chac-mool*, the statue mentioned in *Palomar*. This figure holds a receptacle for the divine offering of the victims' hearts. There is no Mexican teacher in this story to proclaim crushingly, prohibitively, "we don't know what it means." The figure, representative of a messenger of the gods, gives rise to speculation between the couple and their friend as to its significance: Is it a messenger *to* the gods, or a demon *from* the gods? Is it the victim, or the executor of the sacrifice, for all were potentially victims and executors? This inconclusive discussion leads the narrator to penetrate more deeply into his relationship with Olivia. The rather gory image of "i cuori" overlies the more clichéd connotation of the heart as the seat of emotion. The narrator rethinks his role as the one who is eaten, overwhelmed, and dominated, and realizes:

> Il mio torto con Olivia era di considerarmi mangiato da lei, mentre dovevo essere, anzi ero (ero sempre stato) colui che la mangiava. La carne umana più attraente è quella di chi mangia carne umana. Solo nutrendomi voracemente di Olivia non sarei più riuscito insipido al suo palato. (Calvino, *Sotto il sole giaguaro*, p. 54)

> My mistake with Olivia was in considering myself eaten by her, while it should have been me, rather it was (it had always been) me, who was eating her. The most attractive human flesh is that of one who eats human flesh. Only by nourishing myself voraciously on Olivia would I have succeeded in no longer being insipid to her palate.

Through this rather alarming vision, which functions more as a sort of sexual fantasy to even the odds, the themes of gustation, eros, and ancient symbols of life and death become ever more intimately connected.

At dinner, in a reappearance of that transformational humorous element which Calvino uses to restore equilibrium, especially in sexual or other "heavy" discourse, the narrator imagines devouring all of Olivia through the *meatball*, in a sort of gastronomic game of *ménage à trois*: him, Olivia and the meatball.[40] However, a fourth element, essential to the sensibilities of the narrator (and writer), is the *name* of the meatball: *gordita pellizcadas con manteca* (p. 54). The name—like *Oaxaca* at the beginning—works a certain magic, the narrator admits. The name, associated with his discovery of the "parità" between him and Olivia, serves to inspire their first sexual encounter since their arrival in Mexico. The inspiration "che aveva fornito i momenti migliori della nostra convivenza" (that had furnished the best moments of [their] life together) returns (p. 55). It is noteworthy here that the sexual act is not described in detail, but merely mentioned. However, it is clearly presented in a positive light, and lacks the connotations of routine, unexciting lovemaking often associated with extended relationships. The intensity of the eros in this story has certainly been placed—displaced?—within the framework of consumption and degustation and has achieved universal proportions.

The next morning opens onto a very sensual episode that continues to intertwine the story's motifs. The two lovers find themselves in bed in the position of the chac-mool. On their knees is their generic hotel breakfast which they seek to supplement, to save from "insipidness," with luscious-sounding local fruits. They have been ingesting the culture on the voyage and, in a sense, the culture, the atmosphere—suggestive of the past with its ancient rituals and legends—has ingested them; that is, it has been transforming and working its magic on them, and has been in some way reordering and redimensionalizing their dynamic.

This ingestion climaxes in the narrator's climb to the Temple of the Jaguar Sun. At the top, a sense of vertigo takes hold of him, and past and present seem to fuse for him in a moment of danger in which he views himself "sgozzato del coltello del re-sacerdote" (with his throat slit by the knife of the priest-king) and falling amongst the tourists below: "l'energia solare scorreva per reti fittissime di sangue e clorofilla, io vivevo e morivo in tutte le fibre di ciò che viene masticato e digerito" (solar energy flowed in thick networks of blood and chlorophyll; I lived and died in all the fibers of what is chewed and digested—p. 56). The religious cycle of life now merges for the narrator with the biological cycle-of-life construct behind Le cosmicomiche. The biological cycle of life has been expanded to include plants, those edibles that have colored the entire story, and the narrator imagines himself as part of everything he eats, animal and vegetable, on the most literal level.

With his return to Olivia, who had been waiting at the restaurant, the forces of human violence and love are again called into play in the cycle of love and death that characterizes all human interaction. The human cycle of life amounts in the end to the loving and destruction of others. For the narrator, and for Calvino, the balance between eros and death is in equality, "parità," between opponents. At the restaurant, the teeth of both Olivia and the narrator move in "pari ritmo" (equal rhythm), which suggests danger but also a certain harmony and mutual understanding. The image which closes the story is the image of their glances interlocking with the intensity of serpents. It suggests both the cycle that the narrator has been tracing as well as the brutality, the aggression, the risk, involved in living and loving. The two lovers are

> serpenti immedesimati nello spasimo d'inghiottirci a vicenda, coscienti d'essere a nostra volta inghiottiti dal serpente che tutti ci digerisce e assimila incessantemente nel processo d'ingestione e digestione del *cannibalismo* universale che impronta di sé ogni rapporto amoroso e annulla i confini tra i nostri corpi e la *sopa de frijoles*, lo *huacinango a la veracruzana*, le *enchiladas* ... (P. 57, first italics mine)

> serpents absorbed in the spasm of swallowing each other in turn, conscious of being swallowed in turn by the serpent that incessantly digests and assimilates us all in the process of ingestion and digestion of universal *cannibalism* that leaves its mark on every love relation and eliminates the boundaries between our bodies and the *sopa de frijoles*, the *huacinango a la veracruzana*, the *enchiladas* ... (First italics mine)

The individual once again reflects the universal; the relationship becomes a microcosm for universal truths. Personal eros, human eros, i.e., the individual erotic relationship, mirrors all forms of cosmic regeneration and cycles (religious, historical, evolutionary). In this way, the human erotic dimension is redeemed from its most banalizing, stultifying detractors and erotic language is revitalized.

6

Conclusion

This critical reading of Calvino's theoretical and narrative work has sought to underscore the pervasiveness of eros in Calvino's fiction—from his early short stories to *I nostri antenati* to *Le cosmicomiche* and beyond—and its close ties to his theories on language, precision, and individual and societal taboo. At the same time, we have also discovered in several of Calvino's articles a possible explanation for his reluctance to represent eros directly, which in turn may explain the lack of critical attention directed thus far to the theme of eros in his work.

As any serious reader or scholar of Calvino cannot fail to know, this issue, like every other one concerning Calvino's more than four decades of creative experimentations and theorizing, is a complex one and not to be summarily dismissed. A close reading of the erotic dimension, in fact, has revealed Calvino's commitment to representing those exiled realms of the human unconscious which challenge the word to redeem them. As we have seen, Calvino recognizes eros as one of these "unspeakable," ineffable realms.

In Calvino, eros is a powerful force, one that poses a dilemma both in the area of human relations and in the area of literary achievement. In human relations, the dilemma takes the form of a struggle between the erotic as life-affirming and life-threatening, as necessary to individual identity and as dangerous to it. In literature, the dilemma becomes how to represent sexuality positively without falling into cliché. Calvino's grappling with a fresh portrayal of eros in literature is never far from his attempt to understand and revitalize it in human life and within its social context. In a sense, he bridges this grappling between the two worlds, the human and the literary, by the magical, transformational element of laughter, which serves to "lighten" the overwhelming and threatening effects of the erotic life force. His constant reiteration that eros is "sconvolgente," upsetting and unsettling, reveals most clearly his recognition of both the vital and insidious aspects of sexuality, and thus of the delicacy necessary to handle it in the literary work. The best example of the cosmic breadth of the erotic motif in Calvino can be found in "Sotto il sole giaguaro," where the erotic intertwines and mirrors the linguistic, ideological, thematic, and "moral" dimensions of his work.

Perhaps the most appropriate conclusion to our analysis might be a final word on that "battle with language" which Calvino talks about in his *Lezioni americane* and has been, directly and obliquely, addressed in this study. The following passages from his "lectures" of the 1980s seem to echo Calvino's much earlier article "Cibernetica e fantasmi" and conclusively establish Calvino's faith in literature as a unique and essential form of human creation. Calvino concludes "The Written and the Unwritten Word" (1983) thus:

> In a certain way, I think that we always write about something we don't know, we write to give the unwritten world a chance to express itself through us. Yet the moment my attention wanders from the settled order of the written lines to the movable complexity no sentence is able to hold entirely, I come close to understanding that on the other side of words there is something words could mean.[1]

The Italian version of the article adds, "che dall'altro lato delle parole c'è qualcosa che cerca di uscire dal silenzio, di significare attraverso il linguaggio, come battendo su un muro di prigione" (that on the other side of words there is something that seeks to break out of the silence, to mean something through language, as if beating on a prison wall).[2]

In the chapter "Esattezza" in *Lezioni americane*, Calvino explores the "battaglia col linguaggio per farlo diventare il linguaggio delle cose, che parte dalle cose e torna a noi carico di tutto l'umano che abbiamo investito nelle cose" (a battle to force language to become the language of things, starting from things and returning to us changed, with all the humanity we have invested in things).[3] He is affirming the relationship between language and things, redeeming literature's ability to reach outside itself. He says,

> penso che siamo sempre alla caccia di qualcosa di nascosto o di solo potenziale o ipotetico, di cui seguiamo le tracce che affiorano sulla superficie del suolo. *Credo che i nostri meccanismi mentali elementari si ripetono dal Paleolitico dei nostri padri cacciatori e rac-*

coglitori attraverso tutte le culture della storia umana. La parola collega la traccia visibile alla cosa invisibile, alla cosa assente, *alla cosa desiderata o temuta* . . .

Per questo il giusto uso del linguaggio per me è quello che permette di avvicinarsi alle cose (presenti o assenti) con discrezione e attenzione e cautela, col rispetto di ciò che le cose (presenti o assenti) comunicano senza le parole. (Italics mine)

I think we are always searching for something hidden or merely potential or hypothetical, following its traces whenever they appear on the surface. *I think our basic mental processes have come down to us through every period of history, ever since the times of our Paleolithic forefathers who were hunters and gatherers.* The word connects the visible trace with the invisible thing, the absent thing, *the thing that is desired or feared* . . .

For this reason, the proper use of language, for me personally, is one that enables us to approach things (present or absent) with discretion, attention, and caution, with respect for what things (present or absent) communicate without words.[4] (Italics mine)

Notes

Chapter 1. Toward an Understanding of Calvino

1. James Gardner, "Italo Calvino 1923–1985," *New Criterion* 4 (Dec. 1985): 6–13.

2. Albert Howard Carter III, *Italo Calvino: Metamorphoses of Fantasy*, Studies in Speculative Fiction 13 (Ann Arbor, Mich.: UMI Research Press, 1987), 1.

3. Calvino's fiction is provocative especially in light of the imposing aulic literary tradition that precedes him, a tradition that Italian scholars themselves have charged as being too rigid, too bound to classical definitions and rules for literature. De Lauretis, a prominent contemporary scholar of Calvino, states what the Resistance had come to mean for Calvino: "It meant the total renewal of a cultural tradition that had worn itself out and helplessly flown into Fascism . . . At the same time, the Resistance created a new national heritage, the basis of different values, myths, memories and aspirations for the people of Italy. Yet, the real task of Calvino was to recuperate and integrate with the new culture a great literary and popular tradition dating back to the Middle Ages" (Teresa De Lauretis, "Narrative Discourse in Calvino: Praxis or Poiesis?" *PMLA* 90 [May 1975]: 414). Calvino himself confirms in one of his last interviews, granted to Maria Corti, that "riconsiderato il complesso di quel che ho fatto e detto e pensato in bene e in male, devo concludere che la letteratura italiana mi va benissimo e non potrei immaginarmi che nel suo contesto" (considering the entirety of all that I have done and said and thought for better and for worse, I must conclude that Italian literature suits me very well and I could not imagine myself but within its context) (interview of Calvino by Maria Corti, *Autografo* 2 [Oct. 1985]: 53).

4. Italo Calvino, *Se una notte d'inverno un viaggiatore* (Turin: Einaudi, 1979) 9.

5. *Una pietra sopra: Discorsi di letteratura e società* (Turin: Einaudi, 1980) is the most comprehensive collection of Calvino's essays published thus far. *The Uses of Literature* (1986) offers an English translation by Patrick Creagh of some of the essays in *Una pietra sopra*, as well as other essays not found in the 1980 Italian edition.

6. Ian Thomson, "In the Heat of the Moment: A Conversation in Rome with Italo Calvino," *London Magazine*, n.s. 24 (1984–85): 63.

7. Carter, *Italo Calvino*, 157.

8. Calvino, "Tre correnti del romanzo italiano d'oggi," in *Una pietra sopra*, 47.

9. Calvino, "Presentazione," in *Una pietra sopra*, vii.

10. Some of the Calvino's changing perceptions of his own work may also be attributed to a rethinking, repositioning, and retheorizing of his texts. This is reflected in his new editions, new notes, and the occasional reordering of his stories. A prime illustration of this rethinking is explored by Maria Corti

in her well-known study on Marcovaldo in *Il viaggio testuale* (Turin: Einaudi, 1978). Ahern ("Out of Montale's Cave: A Reading of Calvino's *Gli amori difficili*," *Modern Language Studies* 12 ([Winter 1982]) contributes in the same vein to the two orderings and editions of *Gli amori difficili*: 1958 and 1970. Over time, Calvino seems to revaluate his own work in the light of critical and social contexts different from those in which they were written.

11. Renato Barilli, *La barriera del naturalismo*, 3d ed. (Milano: Mursia, 1980), 244.

12. Richard Andrews, "Italo Calvino," in *Writers and Society in Contemporary Italy*, ed. Michael Caesar and Peter Hainsworth (New York: St. Martin's Press, 1984), 259–60.

13. Franco Ricci, "Silence and Loss of Self in Italo Calvino's *Gli amori difficili*," in *The Italianist: Journal of the Department of Italian Studies* 4 (1984): 60.

14. Francesco Guardiani, "Optimism without Illusions," *Review of Contemporary Fiction* 6 (Summer 1986): 58.

15. Ibid., 59.

16. Introduction to *Gli amori difficili*, 2d ed. (Turin: Einuadi, 1970) vii. It is generally accepted that this introduction is by Calvino.

17. De Lauretis, "Narrative Discourse," 414. See note 3 above.

18. Among those many works that deal with fantasy in Calvino are Carter's *Metamorphoses of Fantasy*, Finocchiaro Chimirri's *Italo Calvino tra realtà e favola* and Adler's *Calvino, The Writer as Fablemaker*.

19. These ideas appear to be central to JoAnn Cannon's *Italo Calvino: Writer and Critic* (Ravenna: Longo, 1981). However, several of her more recent articles, such as "Calvino's Latest Challenge to the Labyrinth: A Reading of *Palomar*" (*Italica*, 1985) and "Writing and the Unwritten World in *Sotto il sole giaguaro*" (*Italian Quarterly*, 1989) appear to focus on Calvino's struggle through literature to make sense of the world around him, rather than his belief in literature's inevitable failure to do so.

20. Andrews, "Italo Calvino," 266.

21. Gardner, "Italo Calvino 1923–1985," 10.

22. Giovanni Palmieri, "Calvino: *Una pietra sopra*," *Uomini e libri: Periodico bimestrale di critica ed informazione letteraria* 16 (June–July 1980): 48.

23. Thomson, "In the Heat of the Moment," 67.

24. Calvino had a predilection for short stories, short novels, incipits, and even short prose-poems (*Le città invisibili*). Even his longest text, *Il barone*, is comprised of brief episodes. This seems to me to be an obvious characteristic, and seems not to have drawn much critical attention. However, Calvino briefly mentions his predilection and its importance in the "Rapidità" chapter of *Lezioni americane: Sei proposte per il prossimo millennio* (Milan: Garzanti, 1988), 48. The English version is *Six Memos for the Next Millennium*, trans. Patrick Creagh, (Cambridge: Harvard University Press, 1988).

25. This last is a description De Lauretis uses, applying Greimas's term ("Narrative Discourse," 415).

26. Guido Almansi, "Il mondo binario di Italo Calvino," *Paragone* 22 (1971): 106.

27. I. T. Olken, *With Pleated Eye and Garnet Wing: Symmetries of Italo Calvino* (Ann Arbor: University of Michigan Press, 1984), 73. For a more recent study on "contrast" in Calvino, consult Albert Howard Carter III's "Flaming Crystals: Calvino's Dialectical Imagination (And the Reader's?)," *Italian Quarterly* 115/116 (Winter-Spring 1989): 115–23.

28. De Lauretis, "Narrative Discourse," 415.

29. Olken, *With Pleated Eye*, 27.

30. Tommasina Gabriele, "Literature as Education and the Near-Perfect Protagonist: Narrative Structure in *Il barone rampante*," *Stanford Italian Review* 11:94–95.

31. De Lauretis, "Narrative Discourse," 417.

32. Francesca Bernardini Napoletano, *I segni nuovi di Italo Calvino: Da Le cosmicomiche a Le città invisibili* (Rome: Bulzoni editore s.r.l., 1977), 17–57.

33. Gregorio Scalise, "The Game of Palomar," *Review of Contemporary Fiction* 6 (Summer 1986): 138–45.

34. Giampaolo Dossena, "Sillabari, lipogrammi e rime per l'occhio," in *Italo Calvino—La letteratura la scienza la città: Atti del Convegno nazionale di studi di Sanremo* (1986), ed. Giorgio Bertoni (Genoa: Marietti, 1988), 70–75.

35. Warren F. Motte Jr., "Telling Games," in *Calvino Revisited*, ed. Franco Ricci, University of Toronto Italian Studies 2 (Ottawa: Dovehouse, 1989), 117–30 and "Calvino's Combinatorics," *Review of Contemporary Fiction* 6 (Summer 1986): 81–87.

36. See, for example, Warren Motte's studies on this narrative technique.

37. Olken, *With Pleated Eye*, 20–1.

38. Ibid., 21. In italics: *Una pietra sopra*, 57.

39. Italo Calvino, "The Structure of Orlando Furioso," in *The Uses of Literature*, trans. Patrick Creagh (New York: Harcourt Brace Jovanovich, 1986), 173. This text offers many translations from *Una pietra sopra*, as well as translations from other sources. This particular article is not found in *Una pietra sopra*.

40. Italo Calvino, preface to *Marcovaldo: Ovvero le stagioni in città* (Turin: Einaudi, 1966), 9.

41. Maria Corti, *Il viaggio testuale* (Turin: Einaudi, 1978), 184.

42. Carter, *Metamorphoses*, 73.

43. Luisa Guj, "The Shapeless and the Well-Designed: An Unresolved Dichotomy in Calvino's Narrative?" *Forum for Modern Language Studies* 24 (July 1988): 210.

44. Antonio Illiano, "Per una definizione della vena cosmogonica di Italo Calvino: Appunti su *Le cosmicomiche* e *Ti con zero*," *Italica* 49 (1972): 294.

45. Ibid., 295.

46. Ibid., 294–95.

47. Ibid., 294.

48. Bernardini Napoletano, *I segni nuovi*, 73.

49. Ibid., 74.

50. Claudio Milanini, "Italo Calvino: La trilogia del realismo speculativo," *Belfagor: Rassegna di varia umanità* 44 (31 May 1989): 247.

51. Italo Calvino, "Il midollo del leone," in *Una pietra spra*, 10.

52. Ibid., 13.

53. Italo Calvino, preface to *I nostri antenati* (Turin: Einaudi, 1960) x.

54. Ibid., xi–xii.

55. Barilli, *La barriera*, 246–47.

56. Ibid., 247.

57. Ibid., 252. It must be added that Barilli, in these articles as well as in others, was far from expressing wholehearted praise of *I racconti* and *Le cosmicomiche*. In fact, Barilli specifically condemned Calvino's "sottile ma tenace corazza di buon senso e di normalità" (subtle but tenacious armor of good sense and normality—pp. 251–52), which he felt kept Calvino from completely

immersing himself in his creations. To further explore Barilli's reservations about Calvino's writing and what he preceived as his own influence on Calvino as his critic, see his article, "My 'Long Infidelity' Toward Calvino," in *Calvino Revisited*, ed. Franco Ricci.

58. J. R. Woodhouse, *Italo Calvino: A Reappraisal and an Appreciation of the Trilogy* (Yorkshire: University of Hull, 1968).

59. Donald Heiney, "Calvino and Borges: Some Implications of Fantasy," *Mundus Artium* 2 (1968): 66.

60. Calvino, *Six Memos for the Next Millenium*, trans. Patrick Creagh (Cambridge: Harvard University Press, 1988), 26. All translations will be from *Six Memos* by Creagh unless otherwise stated. The corresponding passage in Italian is in Calvino, *Lezioni americane*, p. 28.

61. Calvino, *Six Memos*, trans. Patrick Creagh, 27. Calvino, *Lezioni americane*, p. 28.

62. De Lauretis, "Narrative Discourse," 414–15.

63. See note 19 above.

64. Riccardo Bruscagli, "Autobiografia (perplessa) di Italo Calvino," *Paragone* 366 (1980): 85–86.

65. Ibid., 86.

66. Ibid., 87.

67. Calvino, "Il midollo," 13.

68. Ibid., 17.

69. Ibid., 18.

70. Italo Calvino, "La sfida al labirinto," in *Una pietra sopra*, 97.

71. We read in this edition: "La prima lezione che potremmo trarre dal libro è che la disobbedienza acquista un senso solo quando diventa una disciplina più rigorosa e ardua di quella a cui si ribella" (The first lesson we can draw from the book is that disobedience acquires a meaning only when it becomes a discipline even more rigorous and arduous than that against which one is rebeling—Tonio Cavilla [Calvino], preface and notes, to *Il barone rampante* by Italo Calvino, [Turin: Einaudi, 1965], 11).

72. Corti interview with Calvino, 49. See note 3.

73. Interview of Italo Calvino by Alexander Stille, *Saturday Review*, April 1985, 39.

74. Vittorio Spinazzola, "L'io diviso di Italo Calvino," *Belfagor: rassegna di varia umanità* 42 (30 Sept. 1987): 529. Also in *Italo Calvino: Atti del convegno a Firenze del 1987*, ed. Giovanni Falaschi (Milan: Garzanti, 1988).

75. Stille interview with Calvino, 39.

76. Franco Ferrucci, in correspondence with the author, 14 October 1990.

77. Jean Michel Gardair, "Lumi e ombre del Settecento," in Bertoni, *Italo Calvino*, 289.

78. Judith Bryce, "Rousseau and Calvino: An Unexplored Ideological Perspective in *Il barone rampante*, in *Moving in measure: Essays in Honor of Brian Moloney*, ed. Judith Bryce and Doug Thompson (Yorkshire: University of Hull Press, 1989), 201.

Chapter 2. An Evolving Theory on the Language of Love

1. Miriam E. Friedman, "Love and Narrative Unity in Calvino," diss., Indiana University, 1983 (Ann Arbor, Mich.: UMI, 1984), microfiche no. 8406799, p. 28.

2. Giovanni Falaschi, ed., *Italo Calvino: Atti del convegno a Firenze del 1987* (Milan: Garzanti, 1988) and Giorgio Bertoni, ed., *Italo Calvino—La letteratura la scienza la città: Atti del Convegno nazionale di studi di Sanremo (1986)* (Genoa: Marietti, 1988).

3. Among the studies that thematically explore love in *Le cosmicomiche* are Kathryn Hume, "Calvino's Framed Narrations: Writers, Readers, and Reality," *Review of Contemporary Fiction*, 6 (1986): 71–80; id., "Italo Calvino's Cosmic Comedy: Mythography for the Scientific Age," *Papers on Language and Literature: A Journal for Scholars and Critics of Language and Literature* 20 (Winter 1984): 80–95; id., "Science and Imagination in Calvino's Cosmicomics," *Mosaic: A Journal for the Interdisciplinary Study of Literature* 15 (Dec. 1982): 47–58; Anca Vlasopolos, "Love and the Two Discourses in *Le cosmicomiche*," *Stanford Italian Review* 4 (Spring 1984): 123–35; John Gery, "Love and Annihilation in Calvino's Qfwfq's Tales," *Critique: Studies in Modern Fiction* 30 (Fall 1988): 59–68.

4. Michael Stephens, "Italo Calvino: A Woman, a Moon, the City," *Review of Contemporary Fiction* 6 (Summer 1986): 70.

5. Mary McCarthy, "Actos de Amor," trans. Millan Montserrat, *Quimera: Revista de Literatura* 20 (June 1982): 32.

6. Albert Howard Carter III, "Italo Calvino: *Metamorphoses of Fantasy*," *Studies in Speculative Fiction* 13 (Ann Arbor, Mich.: UMI Research Press, 1987), 13.

7. Friedman, "Love and Narrative Unity," 28. Cesare Segre, "Se una notte d'inverno uno scrittore sognasse un aleph di dieci colori," *Strumenti critici: Rivista quadrimestrale di cultura e critica letteraria* 39–40 (Oct. 1979): 209.

8. Marilyn Schneider, "Calvino's Erotic Metaphor and the Hermaphroditic Solution," *Stanford Italian Review* 2 (Spring 1981) 93–118. Aurore Frasson-Marin (*Italo Calvino et L'imaginaire* [Paris: Editions Slatkine, 1986]) studies the role of female characters in several of Calvino's novels and the role of the erotic especially in *Le cosmicomiche* and in *Se una notte*, the two works which have drawn the most attention from this perspective.

9. Friedman, "Love and Narrative Unity," 28. Schneider, "Calvino's Erotic Metaphor," 94.

10. Schneider, "Calvino's Erotic Metaphor," 94.

11. Ibid.

12. Teresa De Lauretis, "Calvino and the Amazons Reading the (Post)Modern Text," in *Technologies of Gender: Essays on Theory, Film, and Fiction* (Bloomington: Indiana University Press, 1987), 71.

13. Sara Maria Adler, *Calvino: The Writer as Fablemaker* (Potomac, Md.: José Porrúa Turanzas, S.A., 1979) 126–27.

14. Ibid., 54.

15. Ibid., 55.

16. Pier Vincenzo Mengaldo, "La lingua dello scrittore," in *Italo Calvino: Atti del convegno a Firenze del 1987*.

17. Vittorio Coletti, "Calvino e l'italiano 'concreto' e 'preciso,'" in *Italo Calvino—La letteratura la scienza la città*, 37.

18. Italo Calvino, "L'italiano, una lingua tra le altre," in *Una pietra sopra: Discorsi di letteratura e società* (Turin: Einaudi, 1980), 121.

19. Ibid., 120.

20. Italo Calvino, "L'antilingua," in *Una pietra sopra*, 122–23.

21. Calvino, "L'italiano," 121.

22. Italo Calvino in Giovanna Finocchiaro Chimirri, *Italo Calvino tra realtà e favola* (Catania, Italy: Cooperativa Universitaria Catanese di Magistero, 1987), 97.

23. Interview of Calvino by Maria Corti, *Autografo* 2 (Oct. 1985): 49.

24. Italo Calvino, *Lezioni americane: Sei proposte per il prossimo millennio* (Milan: Garzanti, 1988), 57. In Calvino, *Six Memos for the Next Millenium*, trans. Patrick Creagh (Cambridge: Harvard University Press, 1988), 56.

25. Italo Calvino, "Otto domande sull'erotismo," special issue of *Nuovi Argomenti* 51–52 (July–Oct. 1961). All future references to this article will appear in the text, unless otherwise indicated.

26. Calvino, *Una pietra sopra*, viii.

27. Ibid., footnote on 212.

28. In his interview with Thomson, Calvino comments, "Beckett has a religious, mystical background and is really scared of God . . . For me, religion is just a stimulating game" (p. 66) and "The 'laic', or 'freethinkers' of Italy are much more moralistic than the Catholics. For the free thinker there is only his conscience" (Ian Thomson, "In the Heat of the Moment: A Conversation in Rome with Italo Calvino," *London Magazine*, n.s. 24 [1984–85]: 61).

29. Giovanni Falaschi, "Negli anni del neorealismo," in *Italo Calvino: Atti del convegno a Firenze del 1987*, 116.

30. Ibid., 117.

31. Italo Calvino, *Il visconte dimezzato* (Turin: Einaudi, 1952), 63. All future references will appear in the text and will be taken from this edition, unless otherwise stated.

32. Calvino, *I nostri antenati* (Turin: Einaudi, 1960), xviii. All future references to *Il cavaliere inesistente* will appear in the text and will be taken from this edition, unless otherwise stated.

33. Schneider, "Calvino's Erotic Metaphor," 106.

34. For an exploration of these autobiographical elements, see pages 9, 25 and 38 of J. R. Woodhouse's *Italo Calvino: A Reappraisal and an Appreciation of the Trilogy* as well as his introduction to *Il barone rampante* (Manchester: Manchester University Press, 1970).

35. Italo Calvino, *Il barone rampante* (Turin: Einaudi, 1957), 151–52. All future references will appear in the text and will be taken from this edition, unless otherwise stated.

36. Segre, "Se una notte," 209. To quote just one more example, Benussi, referring to love and death, says that Calvino "rifiuta di parlar[ne]" (refuses to speak of them) and evokes rather than represents these two themes (Benussi, *Introduzione a Calvino* [Roma: Laterza, 1989], 155).

37. Calvino, *I nostri antenati*, x.

38. Italo Calvino, "Definizioni di territori: L'erotico (Il sesso e il riso)," in *Una pietra sopra*. All future references to this article will appear in the text.

39. Italo Calvino, "Cybernetics and Ghosts," in *The Uses of Literature*, trans. Patrick Creagh (New York: Harcourt Brace Jovanovich, 1986), 4. All future references will be taken from this translation by Creagh and will appear in the text, unless otherwise stated. The original is from Italo Calvino, "Cibernetica e fantasmi (Appunti sulla narrativa come processo combinatorio)," in *Una pietra sopra*. Several other English translations of this article have appeared, including "Notes Toward a Definition of the Narrative Form as a Combinative Process" (*Twentieth Century Studies* 3 [May 1970]: 93–101) and, in an abbrevi-

ated form, Raymond Federman, ed., "Myth in the Narrative" in *Surfiction: Fiction Now . . . and Tomorrow* (Chicago: Swallow, 1981).

40. E. H. Gombrich, "Freud e l'arte," in *Freud e la psicologia dell'arte* (Turin: Einaudi, 1967), 28.

41. Ibid., 32.

42. Calvino, *Lezioni americane*, 75. This translation is my own.

43. Simona Di Bucci Felicetti, "Il 'mistero buffo' di Italo Calvino," in *Narrare: Percorsi possibili*, ed. Margherita Di Fazio (Ravenna: Longo, 1989), 209.

44. See Calvino's own declaration of disinterest in "la psicologia" in the preface to the 1960 edition of *I nostri antenati* (p. ix); Pietro Citati's observations, termed positive (by Calvino, we assume) in the "Nota introduttiva" to the 1970 edition of *Gli amori difficili* (p. xiii); and Vittorio Spinazzola's "L'io diviso di Italo Calvino," *Belfagor: Rassegna di varia umanità* 42 (30 Sept. 1987): 529. Also in *Italo Calvino: Atti del convegno a Firenze del 1987*, ed. Giovanni Falaschi (Milan: Garzanti, 1988), 514–15.

45. Gombrich, "Freud e l'arte," 28.

46. Calvino, *The Uses of Literature*, trans. Patrick Creagh, 21–22.

47. Gombrich, "Freud e l'arte," 25.

48. Calvino, *The Uses of Literature*, trans. Patrick Creagh, 22.

49. Calvino, "Il sesso e il riso," 212.

Chapter 3. "Il Movimento a Spirale": Sex, Language and Laughter

1. Teresa De Lauretis, "Narrative Discourse in Calvino: Praxis or Poiesis?" *PMLA* 90 (May 1975): 422.

2. Miriam E. Friedman, "Love and Narrative Unity in Calvino" diss., Indiana University, 1983 (Ann Arbor: UMI, 1984), 98. Microfiche no. 8406799.

3. Italo Calvino, *Cosmicomiche vecchie e nuove* (Milan: Garzanti, 1984), 248. All future references will appear in the text and will be taken from this edition, unless otherwise stated.

4. Italo Calvino, "Definizioni di territori: L'erotico (Il sesso e il riso)," in *Una pietra sopra: Discorsi di letteratura e società* (Turin: Einaudi, 1980), 210.

5. De Lauretis sees in the parallel stories a distinction. She feels that "La spirale" shows human doing, because Qfwfq makes an artistic object, whereas "Mitosis" deals with saying or, to use her terms, poiesis. While "The Spiral" "deals with the human activity of doing (*il fare*), that is to say praxis, "Mitosis" deals with poiesis, or creation by language (*il dire*)" (p. 422). However, one could certainly argue that the spiral is a form of expression, as Qfwfq himself claims, and thus a form of saying, an object as language, as expression and message. Similarly, one could argue that Qfwfq the cell sees his saying as doing and that language in the later story is a metaphor ("Per tornare alla metafora del linguaggio," Qfwfq the cell says—p. 256.) for the genetic and erotic happenings that he is trying to describe. To me the distinction between doing and saying in these stories does not seem to be so clear-cut.

6. See on this point, for example, Asor Rosa's article, "Il 'punto di vista' di Calvino," in *Italo Calvino: Atti del convegno a Firenze del 1987* (Milan: Garzanti, 1988) 261–76 and S.M. Adler's chapter "The Point of View" in *Calvino: The Writer as Fablemaker* (Potomac, Md.: José Porrúa Turanzas, S.A., 1979).

7. Pier Vincenzo Mengaldo, "La lingua dello scrittore," in *Italo Calvino: Atti del convegno a Firenze del 1987* (Milan: Garzanti, 1988), 220.

8. Ibid., 221.

9. Gregory Lucente, "An Interview with Italo Calvino," *Contemporary Literature* (Fall 1984): 253.

10. Ibid.

11. Ibid.

12. This attempt to explain phenomenon is a goal that both literature and science share, Calvino seems to be pointing out, and both are essential—and unique—in their contributions, rather than one being superior to the other. Carter's book—*Italo Calvino: Metamorphoses of Fantasy*, Studies in Speculative Fiction 13 (Ann Arbor, Mich.: UMI Research Press, 1987)—deals with this notion.

13. We do not agree with the assessment of this as "interior lack" in Marilyn Schneider, "Calvino's Erotic Metaphor and the Hermaphroditic Solution," *Stanford Italian Review* 2 (Spring 1981): 95.

14. See, for example, Ahern ("Out of Montale's Cave: A Reading of Calvino's *Gli amori difficili*," *Modern Language Studies* 12 [Winter 1982]: 14–15) and Ricci ("Silence and Loss of Self in Italo Calvino's *Gli amori difficili*," *Italianist: Journal of the Department of Italian Studies* 4 [1984]: 58–59).

15. Italo Calvino, *Gli amori difficili*, 2d ed. (Turin: Einaudi, 1970), 106. All future references will appear in the text and will be taken from this edition, unless otherwise stated.

16. Guido Fink, "Ti con zero," *Paragone* 216 (1968): 151.

17. These characteristics are not to be dismissed as unimportant or typical of reactions to eros. This becomes especially clear if they are compared to other "typical" perceptions of, or reactions to, love, such as disgust, renunciation, and withdrawal, which have been especially common in the twentieth century, as Calvino himself pointed out in his two articles on eros.

18. The instances in which such loss is also represented by the loss of a feminine love object are frequent. Among these, for example, are "Lo zio acquatico," "L'origine degli uccelli," "Senza colori" and "Tutti in un punto."

19. For Lucretius's influence on Calvino on this point, see, for example, Schneider's article and Calvino's own chapter entitled "Leggerezza" in *Lezioni americane*.

20. Hazard Adams, introduction to *Critical Theory Since Plato*, ed. Hazard Adams (New York: Harcourt Brace Jovanovich, 1971), 2.

21. "Calvino measures the scientific universe, using humanity as his yardstick. He manages to retain an undaunted sense of man's significance despite the immensity of the cosmos. He affirms man's stature without denying his triviality as a scientific phenomenon and without artificially dwarfing the scale of the natural universe. He looks at mankind without idealizing its representatives, and yet does not find them wanting. The result is a universe in which Pascal's infinite, silent spaces are filled with human—and humane—warmth (Hume, "Italo Calvino's Cosmic Comedy: Mythography for the Scientific Age," *Papers on Language and Literature: A Journal for Scholars and Critics of Language and Literature* 20 [Winter 1984]: 81). Along these same lines, we read Guj's comment, "The physical world, without a consciousness to interpret it, would have no meaning" (Guj, "The Shapeless and the Well-Designed: An

Unresolved Dichotomy in Calvino's Narrative?" *Forum for Modern Language Studies* 24 [July 1988]: 213).

22. Mengaldo, "La lingua dello scrittore," 221.

Chapter 4. Another Interpretation of *Gli amori difficili*

1. Italo Calvino, "Nota introduttiva," in "Gli amori difficili," 2d ed. (Turin: Einaudi, 1970), x. All future references will appear in the text and will be taken from this edition, unless otherwise stated.

2. Franco Ricci, "Introversion and Effacement in *I racconti* of Italo Calvino," *Italica* 63 (Winter 1986): 351.

3. Miriam E. Friedman, "Love and Narrative Unity in Calvino," diss., Indiana University, 1983 (Ann Arbor: UMI, 1984), 161. Microfiche no. 8406799.

4. Some of the stories of *Ultimo viene il corvo* were published in newspapers. We refer to Calvino's note to the 1969 edition of this text, as well as to Falaschi's article, "Negli anni del neorealismo," in *Italo Calvino: Atti del convegno a Firenze del 1987*, ed. Giovanni Falaschi (Milan: Garzanti, 1988).

5. Markey, in her unpublished dissertation, as quoted by Ricci, says that the characters are "so deprived of humanity as to play the spectator even in moments of the greatest intimacy" (Ricci, "Silence and Loss of Self in Italo Calvino's *Gli amori difficili*," *Italianist: Journal of the Department of Italian Studies* 4 [1984]: 71).

6. Renato Barilli, *La barriera del naturalismo*, 3d ed. (Milano: Mursia editore, 1980), 242–44.

7. Ibid., 245.

8. Ibid., 244.

9. Ibid.

10. Ibid., 245–46.

11. Friedman, "Love and Narrative Unity," 122.

12. Ibid., 153–54

13. Ricci, "Introversion," 340.

14. Ricci, "Silence," 54.

15. Ibid., 55.

16. Ibid., 54.

17. Ibid., 55.

18. See note 6 to chapter 3.

19. We recall Qfwfq's "innamoramento di sé" and sense of plenitude. An investigation of the role of "narcissism" in these texts might prove illuminating.

20. Italo Calvino, "Otto domande sull'erotismo," special issue of *Nuovi Argomenti* 51–52 (July–Oct. 1961): 24.

21. Consult the first chapter of this book, as well as note 18 to chapter 1.

22. Friedman, "Love and Narrative Unity," 161.

23. Ricci, "Silence," 55.

24. John Ahern, "Out of Montale's Cave: A Reading of Calvino's *Gli amori difficili*," *Modern Language Studies* 12 (Winter 1982): 3.

25. Friedman, "Love and Narrative Unity," 123.

26. Italo Calvino, "L'avventura di un soldato," *Ultimo viene il corvo* (Turin: Einaudi, 1949): 230.

27. For a brief analysis of the film that was based on this story, as well as

for some considerations on eros, mystery and humor in Calvino's work, see Di Bucci Felicetti's article "Il 'mistero buffo' di Italo Calvino," in *Narrare: Percorsi possibili*, ed. Margherita Di Fazio (Ravenna: Longo, 1989).

28. We find elements of one story picked up and reworked differently in another story, and this is probably what the "Nota introduttiva" is referring to when it mentions the "gioco combinatorio."

29. *Oxford Abridged English Dictionary*, 1989 ed., s.v. "Bikini."

30. Calvino, "Otto domande," 21.

31. Ahern, "Out of Montale's Cave," 3.

32. Ibid., 7.

33. Friedman, "Love and Narrative Unity," 134.

34. Ibid., 132.

35. Ibid., 133.

36. Italo Calvino, "Definizioni di territori: L'erotico (Il sesso e il riso)," in *Una pietra sopra: Discorsi di letteratura e società* (Turin: Einaudi, 1980), 212.

37. Ahern, "Out of Montale's Cave," 14.

38. For example, the descriptions of the sexual episodes between Cosimo and Violante are rendered poetically and the love scene between "il lettore" and "la lettrice" is described through the metaphor of reading. However, one of the few sexually explicit episodes can be found in *Se una notte*, in the story "Sul tappeto di foglie illuminate dalla luna" (Turin: Einaudi, 1979), 207–9.

39. See note 10 to chapter 1.

40. Teresa De Lauretis, "Calvino and the Amazons," in *Technologies of Gender Essays on Theory, Film, and Fiction* (Bloomington: Indiana University Press, 1987), 71.

41. Calvino, "Otto domande," 24.

42. Ibid.

43. Italo Calvino, "The Written and the Unwritten Word," trans. William Weaver, *New York Review of Books* 12 (May 1983): 38. Later reprinted as "Mondo scritto e mondo non scritto," in *Lettera internazionale* 4–5 (1985): 17.

Chapter 5. Preserving the Self and Tearing the Other to Pieces

1. Some of Calvino's neorealist works, such as *Il sentiero dei nidi di ragno*, show love to be a negative, destructive human experience, but this may be in adherence to neorealist approaches to eros.

2. Vittorio Spinazzola, "L'io diviso di Italo Calvino," *Belfagor: Rassegna di varia umanità* 42 (30 Sept. 1987): 515. Also in *Italo Calvino—La letteratura la scienza la città: Atti del Convegno nazionale di studi di Sanremo* (1986), ed. Giorgio Bertoni (Genoa: Marietti, 1988).

3. These interviews were later published in A. Sinigaglia's *Vent'anni al Duemila* and reproduced as well in Finocchiaro-Chimirri, *Italo Calvino tra realtà e favola* (Catania, Italy: Cooperativa Universitaria Catanese di Magistero, 1987). All future references will appear in the text and will be taken from the latter edition.

4. Calvino does not, however, pursue this complex and provocative train of thought to specify exactly what these differences are.

5. Parts of the following analysis of *Il barone rampante* are taken from my "Literature as Education and the Near-Perfect Protagonist: Narrative Structure

in *Il barone rampante,*" *Stanford Italian Review* 11: 91–102. It is included here thanks to the kind permission of the *Stanford Italian Review.* Please consult this article for a more in-depth explanation of the likeness-contrast technique. An earlier version of this research was presented at the thirteenth Annual Colloquium on Literature and Film, held at the West Virginia University in 1988.

6. Among these are Marilyn Miguel, "The Phantasm of Omnipotence in Calvino's Trilogy," *Modern Language Studies* 16 (Summer 1986): 57–68) and Giuliana Sanguinetti Katz, "Le 'adolescenze difficili' di Italo Calvino," *Quaderni d'Italianistica: Official Journal of the Canadian Society for Italian Studies* 2 (Autumn 1984): 247–61).

7. Tonio Cavilla (Calvino), preface and notes to *Il barone rampante* by Italo Calvino (Turin: Einaudi, 1965), 10.

8. J. R. Woodhouse, introduction and notes to *Il barone rampante* by Italo Calvino (Manchester: Manchester University Press, 1970), p. xxvii.

9. Italo Calvino, *The Baron in the Trees,* trans. Archibald Colquhoun (New York: Random House, 1959), 64.

10. Calvino, *Il barone* (1965), 149.

11. Adler (*Calvino: The Writer as Fablemaker* [Potomac, Md.: José Porrúa Turanzas, S.A., 1979], 75) directs the reader to Calvino's "Lettera a Mario Boselli" (*Nuova corrente* [1964]: 108). Adler suggests that the notes to the 1965 edition provide such an analysis, while our own study reveals that there is much yet to be discovered. The silence of the critics on this structure further corroborates our conviction that little attention has, in fact, been given to this technique. Please consult "Literature as Education and the Near-Perfect Protagonist: Narrative Structure in *Il barone rampante,*" *Stanford Italian Review* 11: 91–102 for a more in-depth explanation of the likeness-contrast technique.

12. Jill Margo Carlton also sees this allusion to the Book of Genesis in her article, "The Genesis of *Il barone rampante,*" *Italica* 61 (Autumn 1984): 204–5.

13. Italo Calvino, *Il barone rampante* (Turin: Einaudi, 1957), 187. All future references will appear in the text and will be taken from this edition, unless otherwise stated.

14. Contardo Calligaris, *Italo Calvino* (Milan: Mursia, 1973), 54.

15. Italo Calvino, *Il castello dei destini incrociati* (Turin: Einaudi, 1973), 85.

16. Northrop Frye, *Anatomy of Criticism: Four Essays* (New York: Atheneum, 1957), 105–6. Quoted in Italo Calvino, "La letteratura come proiezione del desiderio (Per l' *Anatomia della critica* di Northrop Frye," in *Una pietra sopra: Discorsi di letteratura e società* (Turin: Einaudi, 1980), 195–96.

17. Frye, *Anatomy of Criticism,* 106.

18. Another indication of his preference for Cosimo's view can be found in his preface to the 1960 edition of *I nostri antenati,* in which Violante is "a contrasto con la determinatezza illuminista, la spinta barocca e poi romantica verso il tutto che rischia sempre di diventare spinta distruttiva, corsa verso il nulla" (in contrast to Enlightenment determination, the Baroque and then Romantic drive toward the all that always risks becoming destructive, a rush towards nothingness—p. xv).

19. Italo Calvino, *Sotto il sole giaguaro* (Milan: Garzanti, 1983).

20. Critics are divided as to whether it is an ultimately positive or negative image of the "observer" Palomar that Calvino gives. For example, John Hannay rejects Ricci's assessment of Palomar as "cynical, misanthropic, nihilistic": "In characterizing Palomar's solitude as nihilistic . . . Ricci misses the redemptive

value of Palomar's probing, humorous self-reflections" ("Description as Science and Art: Calvino's Narrative of Observation," *Mosaic: A Journal for the Interdisciplinary Study of Literature* 21 [Fall 1988]: 84). See also Richard Grigg's article "Language, the Other, and God: On Italo Calvino's Last Novels," in *Religion and Literature* 19 [Autumn 1987]: 49–65 and Cannon's study of *Palomar* ("Calvino's Latest Challenge to the Labyrinth: A Reading of *Palomar*," *Italica*, 62 [Autumn 1985]: 189–200).

21. Italo Calvino, *Mr. Palomar*, trans. William Weaver (New York: Harcourt Brace Jovanovich, 1985), 20–21. All future references will appear in the text and will be taken from Weaver's translation, unless otherwise indicated. The original Italian was in *Palomar* (Turin: Einaudi, 1983), 22–23.

22. Calvino, "Il sesso e il riso," 213n.

23. Ibid., 214.

24. Perhaps a fuller exploration of Borges's influence on this point, not to be undertaken here, might produce further enlightenment. While the relation between Borges and Calvino has been hinted at and broached by a few critics, and although the influence of Borges on Calvino has been recognized by a number of Calvino scholars, a thorough investigation seems to be lacking. It is interesting to note, for example, as a sign of the validity of such an investigation, that the definition of the Aleph by Borges as "todos in un punto" becomes the title for one story of *Le cosmicomiche*: "Tutto in un punto." ("Aclaró que un Aleph es uno de los puntos del espacio que contienen todos los puntos" (See Jorge Luis Borges, "El Aleph," *Antología personal* [Buenos Aires: Sur, 1961], 142.) However, there are also many differences between the two authors, among the most important of which is the use of humor in sexual representation characteristic of Calvino.

25. Marilyn Schneider has recently explored this connection in her article "Indistinct Boundaries: Calvino's Taste for Otherness," *Italian Quarterly* 115/116 (Winter-Spring 1989): 101–13.

26. Calvino, in interview by Lucente, 250.

27. Ibid., 251.

28. Calvino, *Sotto il sole giaguaro*, 29. All future references, unless otherwise indicated, will appear in the text and will be taken from this 1986 edition. Unless otherwise indicated, the translation will be my own.

29. Calvino, *Under the Jaguar Sun*, trans. William Weaver (New York: Harcourt Brace Jovanovich, 1988), 3.

30. Calvino, "The Written and the Unwritten Word," trans. William Weaver, *New York Review of Books* 12 (May 1983): 39. JoAnn Cannon also explores the connection between *Sotto il sole giaguaro* and this article in "Writing and the Unwritten World in *Sotto il sole giaguaro*," *Italian Quarterly* 115–16 (Winter-Spring 1989): 93–99.

31. Calvino, "The Written and the Unwritten Word," 39.

32. Once again, this erotic dimension draws scant attention from critics.

33. "Sua moglie è argentina, d'origine russa, traduttrice dall'inglese" (His wife is Argentine, of Russian origin, an English translator) (Giuseppe Bonura, *Invito alla lettura di Calvino* [Milan: Mursia, 1972], 40).

34. For more examples, see Calvino, *Sotto il sole giaguro*, 52.

35. Niccolò Tommaseo, *Dizionario dei sinonimi della lingua italiana*, ed. Paolo Ghiglieri, 4 vols. (Florence: Vallecchi Editore, 1973), 1706–7.

36. Schneider also mentions the connection between eating and travel which

is central to the story: "To experience pre-Columbian culture, the couple must experience the great variety of Mexican spices" ("Indistinct Boundaries," 110).

37. Calvino, "Otto domande sull'erotismo," special issue of *Nuovi Argomenti* 51–52 (July-Oct. 1961): 24.

38. Alonso himself is a symbol of continuity between civilizations, for the narrator, in attributing a genealogy to him, writes that he might be "olmeche (o mixteche? o zapoteche?)" (p. 40).

39. Calvino, *The Uses of Literature*, trans. Patrick Creagh (New York: Harcourt Brace Jovanovich, 1986), 19. See chapter 2, n. 39 for further information.

40. "Heaviness" is contrasted to the characteristic of "lightness," which Calvino asserts he prefers, in the eponymous chapter of *Lezioni americane*.

Chapter 6. Conclusion

1. Calvino, trans. William Weaver. "The Written and the Unwritten Word," 39.

2. Calvino, "Mondo scritto e mondo non scritto," 18. My translation.

3. Calvino, *Six Memos*, trans. Creagh, 76. The Italian can be found in *Lezioni americane*, 73–74.

4. Calvino, *Six Memos*, trans. Creagh, 77. The Italian can be found in *Lezioni americane*, 74–75.

Selected Bibliography

Primary Sources

Calvino, Italo. *Gli amori difficili.* 2d ed. Turin: Einaudi, 1970.

―――. "L'avventura di un soldato." In *Ultimo viene il corvo,* 221–34. Turin: Einaudi, 1949.

―――. *Il barone rampante.* Preface and notes by Tonio Cavilla [Italo Calvino]. Special edition. Letture per le scuole medie. Turin: Einaudi, 1965.

―――. *Il barone rampante.* Turin: Einaudi, 1957.

―――. *The Baron in the Trees.* Translated by Archibald Colquhoun. New York: Random House, 1959.

―――. *Il castello dei destini incrociati.* Turin: Einaudi, 1973.

―――. *Le città invisibili.* Turin: Einaudi, 1972.

―――. *Collezione di sabbia.* Milano: Garzanti, 1984.

―――. *Cosmicomiche vecchie e nuove.* Milan: Garzanti, 1984.

―――. "Definizioni di territori: l'erotico (Il sesso e il riso)." In *Una pietra sopra: Discorsi di letteratura e società,* 211–14. Turin: Einaudi, 1980.

―――. *L'entrata in guerra.* Turin: Einaudi, 1954.

―――. *Fiabe italiane.* 2 vols. Milan: Mondadori, 1981.

―――. "Lettera a Mario Boselli." *Nuova corrente* (1964): 102–10.

―――. *Lezioni americane: Sei proposte per il prossimo millennio.* Milan: Garzanti, 1988.

―――. *I libri degli altri.* Turin: Einaudi, 1991.

―――. Preface to *Marcovaldo: Ovvero le stagioni in città.* Turin: Einaudi, 1966.

―――. *Mr. Palomar.* Translated by William Weaver. New York: Harcourt Brace Jovanovich, 1985.

―――. "Mondo scritto e mondo non scritto." *Lettera Internazionale* 4–5 (1985): 16–18.

―――. "Myth in the Narrative." In *Surfiction: Fiction Now . . . and Tomorrow,* edited by Raymond Federman, 75–81. Chicago: Swallow Press, Inc., 1975.

―――. *I nostri antenati.* Turin: Einaudi, 1960.

―――. "Nota introduttiva." In *Gli amori difficili.* 2d ed. Turin: Einuadi, 1958. It is generally accepted that this introduction is by Calvino.

―――. *La nuvola di smog e la formica argentina.* Turin: Einaudi, 1958.

―――. "On Kundera." *Review of Contemporary Fiction* 9 (Summer 1989): 53–57.

―――. *Orlando furioso di Ludovico Ariosto raccontato da Italo Calvino.* Turin: Einaudi, 1970.

————. [Otto domande sull'erotismo]. *Nuovi Argomenti* 51–52 (July–Oct. 1961): 21–24. (Special issue.)

————. *Palomar.* Turin: Einaudi, 1983.

————. "Popular Traditions in Folktales." *Russian Literature* 12 (July 1982): 57–70.

————. *I racconti.* Turin: Einaudi, 1958.

————. "Sade Is Within Us." *Stanford Italian Review* 2 (Fall 1982): 107–11.

————. *Il sentiero dei nidi di ragno.* Turin: Einaudi, 1964.

————. *Se una notte d'inverno un viaggiatore.* Turin: Einaudi, 1979.

————. *Six Memos for the Next Millennium.* Trans. Patrick Creagh. Cambridge: Harvard University Press, 1988.

————. *Sotto il sole giaguaro.* Milan: Garzanti, 1986.

————. *La strada di San Giovanni.* Milan: Mondadori, 1990.

————. *Ultimo viene il corvo.* Turin: Einaudi, 1949.

————. *Una pietra sopra: Discorsi di letteratura e società.* Turin: Einaudi, 1980.

————. *Under the Jaguar Sun.* Translated by William Weaver. New York: Harcourt Brace Jovanovich, 1988.

————. *The Uses of Literature.* Translated by Patrick Creagh. New York: Harcourt Brace Jovanovich, 1986. Contains translations of some articles from *Una pietra sopra,* as well as of other articles.

————. *Il visconte dimezzato.* Turin: Einaudi, 1952.

————. "The Written and the Unwritten Word." Translated by William Weaver. *New York Review of Books* 12 (May 1983): 38–39.

Interviews Cited

Corti, Maria. "Intervista a Italo Calvino." *Autografo* 2 (Oct. 1985): 47–53.

Lucente, Gregory. "An Interview with Italo Calvino." *Contemporary Literature* (Fall 1984): 245–53.

Stille, Alexander. "An Interview with Italo Calvino." *Saturday Review,* April 1985, 37–39.

Thomson, Ian. "In the Heat of the Moment: A Conversation in Rome with Italo Calvino." *London Magazine,* n.s. 24 (1984–85): 54–68.

Secondary Sources Cited

Adams, Hazard. Introduction to *Critical Theory Since Plato.* Edited by Hazard Adams. New York: Harcourt Brace Jovanovich, 1971.

Adler, Sara Maria. *Calvino: The Writer as Fablemaker.* Potomac, Md.: José Porrúa Turanzas, 1979.

Ahern, John. "Out of Montale's Cave: A Reading of Calvino's *Gli amori difficili.*" *Modern Language Studies* 12 (Winter 1982): 3–19.

Almansi, Guido. "Il mondo binario di Italo Calvino." *Paragone* 22 (1971): 95–110.

Andrews, Richard. "Italo Calvino." In *Writers and Society in Contemporary*

Italy, edited by Michael Caesar and Peter Hainsworth, 259–81. New York: St. Martin's Press, 1984.

Asor Rosa, Alberto. "Il 'punto di vista' di Calvino." In *Italo Calvino: Atti del convegno a Firenze del 1987*, edited by Giovanni Falaschi, 261–76. Milan: Garzanti, 1988.

Barilli, Renato. *La barriera del naturalismo*. 3d ed. Milano: Mursia, 1980.

———. "My 'Long Infidelity' Toward Calvino." In *Calvino Revisited*, edited by Franco Ricci, 9–16. University of Toronto Italian Studies 2. Ottawa: Dovehouse, 1989.

Benussi, Cristina. *Introduzione a Calvino*. Roma: Laterza, 1989.

Bernardini Napoletano, Francesca. *I segni nuovi di Italo Calvino: Da Le cosmicomiche a Le città invisibili*. Rome: Bulzoni, 1977.

Bonura, Giuseppe. *Invito alla lettura di Calvino*. Milan: Mursia, 1972.

Borges, Jorge Luis. "El Aleph." In *Antología personal*, 135–49. Buenos Aires: Sur, 1961.

Bruscagli, Riccardo. "Autobiografia (perplessa) di Italo Calvino," *Paragone* 366 (1980): 82–87.

Bryce, Judith. "Rousseau and Calvino: An Unexplored Ideological Perspective in *Il barone rampante*." *Moving in Measure: Essays in Honor of Brian Moloney*. Edited by Judith Bryce and Doug Thompson, 201–14. Yorkshire: University of Hull Press, 1989.

Calligaris, Contardo. *Italo Calvino*. Milan: Mursia, 1973.

Cannon, JoAnn. *Italo Calvino: Writer and Critic*. Ravenna: Longo, 1981.

———. "Calvino's Latest Challenge to the Labyrinth: A Reading of *Palomar*." *Italica* 62 (Autumn 1985): 189–200.

———. *Postmodern Italian Fiction: The Crisis of Reason in Calvino, Eco, Sciascia, Malerba*. Teaneck, N.J.: Fairleigh Dickinson University Press, 1989.

———. "Writing and the Unwritten World in *Sotto il sole giaguaro*." *Italian Quarterly* 115–116 (Winter–Spring 1989): 93–99.

Carlton, Jill Margo. "The Genesis of *Il barone rampante*." *Italica* 61 (Autumn 1984): 195–206.

Carter, Albert Howard III. "Flaming Crystals: Calvino's Dialectical Imagination (And the Reader's?)." *Italian Quarterly* 115–116 (Winter–Spring 1989): 115–23.

———. *Italo Calvino: Metamorphoses of Fantasy*. Studies in Speculative Fiction 13. Ann Arbor, Mich.: UMI Research Press, 1987.

Coletti, Vittorio. "Calvino e l'italiano 'concreto' e 'preciso.'" In *Italo Calvino— La letteratura la scienza la città: Atti del Convegno nazionale di studi di Sanremo (1986)*, edited by Giorgio Bertoni, 36–43. Genoa: Marietti, 1988.

Corti, Maria. *Il viaggio testuale*. Turin: Einaudi, 1978.

De Lauretis, Teresa. "Calvino and the Amazons." In *Technologies of Gender Essays on Theory, Film, and Fiction*, 70–83. Bloomington: Indiana University Press, 1987.

———. "Narrative Discourse in Calvino: Praxis or Poiesis?" *PMLA* 90 (May 1975): 414–25.

Di Bucci Felicetti, Simona. "Il 'mistero buffo' di Italo Calvino." In *Narrare*:

percorsi possibili, edited by Margherita Di Fazio, 204–14. Ravenna: Longo editore, 1989.

Dossena, Giampaolo. "Sillabari, lipogrammi e rime per l'occhio." In *Italo Calvino—La letteratura la scienza la città: Atti del Convegno nazionale di studi di Sanremo (1986)*, edited by Giorgio Bertoni, 70–75. Genoa: Marietta, 1988.

Falaschi, Giovanni. "Negli anni del neorealismo." In *Italo Calvino Atti del convegno a Firenze del 1987*, edited by Giovanni Falaschi, 113–40. Milan: Garzanti, 1988.

Ferrucci, Franco. Letter to author, 14 October 1990.

Fink, Guido. "Ti con zero." *Paragone* 216 (1968): 149–53.

Finocchiaro-Chimirri, Giovanna. *Italo Calvino tra realità e favola.* Catania: Cooperativa Universitaria Catanese di Magistero, 1987.

Frasson-Marin, Aurore. *Italo Calvino et l'imaginaire.* Paris: Slatkine, 1986.

Friedman, Miriam E. "Love and Narrative Unity in Calvino." Diss., Indiana University, 1983. Ann Arbor: UMI, 1984. Microfiche no. 8406799.

Frye, Northrop. *Anatomy of Criticism: Four Essays.* New York: Atheneum, 1957.

Gabriele, Tommasina. "Literature as Education and the Near-Perfect Protagonist: Narrative Structure in *Il barone rampante*." *Stanford Italian Review* 11:91–102.

Gardair, Jean Michel. "Lumi e ombre del Settecento." *Italo Calvino: Atti del convegno a Firenze del 1987*, edited by Giovanni Falaschi, 289–96. Milan: Garzanti, 1988.

Gardner, James. "Italo Calvino 1923–1985." *New Criterion* 4 (Dec. 1985): 6–13.

Gery, John. "Love and Annihilation in Calvino's Qfwfq's Tales." *Critique: Studies in Modern Fiction* 30 (Fall 1988): 59–68.

Gombrich, E. H. "Freud e l'arte." *Freud e la psicologia dell'arte*, 13–40. Turin: Einaudi, 1967.

Guardiani, Francesco. "Optimism without Illusions." *Review of Contemporary Fiction* 6 (Summer 1986): 54–61.

Guj, Luisa. "The Shapeless and the Well-Designed: An Unresolved Dichotomy in Calvino's Narrative?" *Forum for Modern Language Studies* 24 (July 1988): 206–17.

Hannay, John. "Description as Science and Art: Calvino's Narrative of Observation." *Mosaic: A Journal for the Interdisciplinary Study of Literature* 21 (Fall 1988): 73–86.

Heiney, Donald. "Calvino and Borges: Some Implications of Fantasy." *Mundus Artium* 2 (1968): 66–76.

Hume, Kathryn. "Calvino's Framed Narrations: Writers, Readers, and Reality." *Review of Contemporary Fiction* 6 (1986): 71–80.

———. "Italo Calvino's Cosmic Comedy: Mythography for the Scientific Age." *Papers on Language and Literature: A Journal for Scholars and Critics of Language and Literature* 20 (Winter 1984): 80–95.

———. "Science and Imagination in Calvino's *Cosmicomics*." *Mosaic: A Journal for the Interdisciplinary Study of Literature* 15 (Dec. 1982): 47–58.

Illiano, Antonio. "Per una definizione della vena cosmogonica di Italo Calvino: Appunti su *Le cosmicomiche* e *Ti con zero*." *Italica* 49 (1972): 191–301.

McCarthy, Mary. "Actos de Amor." Translated by Millan Montserrat. *Quimera: Revista de Literatura* 20 (June 1982): 32–35.

Mengaldo, Pier Vincenzo. "La lingua dello scrittore." In *Italo Calvino Atti del convegno a Firenze del 1987*, edited by Giovanni Falaschi, 203–24. Milan: Garzanti, 1988.

Miguel, Marilyn. "The Phantasm of Omnipotence in Calvino's Trilogy." *Modern Language Studies* 16 (Summer 1986): 57–68.

Milanini, Claudio. "Italo Calvino: La trilogia del realismo speculativo." *Belfagor: Rassegna di varia umanità* 44 (31 May 1989): 241–62.

———. *L'utopia discontinua: Saggi su Italo Calvino*. Milan: Garzanti, 1990.

Motte, Warren F., Jr. "Calvino's Combinatorics." *Review of Contemporary Fiction* 6 (Summer 1986): 81–87.

———. "Telling Games." In *Calvino Revisited*, edited by Franco Ricci, 117–30. University of Toronto Italian Studies 2. Ottawa: Dovehouse, 1989.

Olken, I. T. *With Pleated Eye and Garnet Wing: Symmetries of Italo Calvino*. Ann Arbor: University of Michigan Press, 1984.

Oxford Abridged English Dictionary, 1989, s.v. "Bikini."

Palmieri, Giovanni. "Calvino: Una pietra sopra." *Uomini e libri: Periodico bimestrale di critica ed informazione letteraria* 16 (June–July 1980): 48.

Ricci, Franco. *Difficult Games: A Reading of "I racconti" by Italo Calvino*. Waterloo, Ont.: Wilfred Laurier University Press, 1990.

———. "Introversion and Effacement in *I racconti* of Italo Calvino." *Italica* 63 (Winter 1986): 331–45.

———. "Silence and Loss of Self in Italo Calvino's *Gli amori difficili*." *Italianist: Journal of the Department of Italian Studies* (1984): 54–72.

Sanguinetti Katz, Giuliana. "Le 'adolescenze difficili' di Italo Calvino." *Quaderni d'Italianistica: Official Journal of the Canadian Society for Italian Studies* 2 (Autumn 1984): 247–261.

Scalise, Gregorio. "The Game of Palomar." *Review of Contemporary Fiction* 6 (Summer 1986): 138–45.

Schneider, Marilyn. "Calvino's Erotic Metaphor and the Hermaphroditic Solution." *Stanford Italian Review* 2 (Spring 1981): 93–118.

———. "Indistinct Boundaries: Calvino's Taste for Otherness." *Italian Quarterly* 115–116 (Winter–Spring 1989): 101–13.

Segre, Cesare. "Se una notte d'inverno uno scittore sognasse un aleph di dieci colori." *Strumenti critici: Rivista quadrimestrale di cultura e critica letteraria* 39–40 (Oct. 1979): 177–214.

Spinazzola, Vittorio. "L'io diviso di Italo Calvino." *Belfagor: Rassegna di varia umanità* 42 (30 Sept. 1987): 507–31. Also in *Italo Calvino: Atti del convegno a Firenze del 1987*, edited by Giovanni Falaschi, 514–15. (Milan: Garzanti, 1988).

Stephens, Michael. "Italo Calvino: A Woman, a Moon, the City." *Review of Contemporary Fiction* 6 (Summer 1986): 62–70.

Tommaseo, Niccolò. *Dizionario dei sinonimi della lingua italiana*. Edited by Paolo Ghiglieri. 4 vols. Florence: Vallecchi, 1973.

Vlasopolos, Anca. "Love and the Two Discourses in *Le cosmicomiche*. *Stanford Italian Review* **4** (Spring 1984): 123–35.

Woodhouse, J. R. Introduction to *Il barone rampante*. Manchester: Manchester University Press, 1970.

————. *Italo Calvino: A Reappraisal and an Appreciation of the Trilogy*. Yorkshire: University of Hull, 1968.

Index

Absence: in love, 38, 39, 84, 109, 112, 127

Adler, Sara Maria: on *Barone rampante*, 122; on love, 38–39

Ahern, John: on "Avventura di una bagnante," 110; on "Avventura di una moglie," 103; on "Avventura di un soldato," 96; on routine, 110

Almansi, Guido, 18

Amori difficili, Gli, 38, 39, 70, 77–78, 89–116; *ars combinatoria* in, 109; beginnings of love stories in, 70; De Lauretis on, 112; erotic detail in, 53, 93–94; fantasy in, 94; Friedman on, 90, 92, 93–94, 103; "morale" in, 91; movement in, 93; objects in, 92; "Nota introduttiva" of, 106, 107, 111–13; Ricci on, 92–93; routine in, 109–10; silence in, 111–16; and "straniamento," 109, 110; variants in, 47. *See also under titles of "Avventure"*

Andrews, Richard, 16, 17, 29

Ariosto, Ludovico, 20–21, 49; and *Barone rampante*, 124; and games, 20–21

Ars Combinatoria, 36, 57, 62, 76, 77, 83; in *Amori difficili*, 109, 161 n.28

"Avventura di due sposi," 109–11; routine in, 110

"Avventura di un automobilista," 77–78

"Avventura di una bagnante," 94–95, 98; Ahern on, 110; and Freud, 100; and narcissism, 100, 101; and nudity, 98–101; and relationship to the body, 98–101; and sin, 100; taboos in, 99

"Avventura di una moglie," 102–3; Ahern on, 103; Friedman on, 103; and identity, 102–3; narcissism in, 102; plenitude in, 102; similarities to "Avventura di un impiegato," 102, 103; taboo in, 102

"Avventura di un impiegato," 95, 103–7; communication in, 106; fantasy in, 95; and mediocrity, 104–5; routine in, 110; and "Sesso e il riso," 106; similarities to "Aventura di una moglie," 102, 103; similarities to "Avventura di un viaggiatore," 106–7

"Avventura di un poeta," 98–99, 112–18, 145; Ahern on, 96; erotic detail in, 95–98, 115; fantasy in, 94; Friedman on, 96; and "Sesso e il riso," 114; silence in, 115

"Avventura di un soldato," 94, 95–98; sexual bildungsroman in, 95; sexual odyssey in, 97; variants in, 97

"Avventura di un viaggiatore," 107–9; plenitude in, 107–9; routine in, 110; similarities to "Avventura di un impiegato," 106–7

Barilli, Renato, 16; on engagement, 27–28; on "the gaze," 90–92; on *Racconti*, 90–92, 93, 154–55 n.57

Barone rampante, 31, 120, 121–25, 126, 133; Adler on, 122; and Ariosto, 124; contrast in, 19; and Diderot, 34; eros in, 127–28; erotic detail in, 51–53; individual identity in, 121, 123; jealousy in, 123–24; and French Enlightenment, 34; Guardini on, 16; introduction to, 15; and love story, 38, 39; madness in, 124–25; middle school edition of, 14; "morale" in, 32, 121, 124; narrative structure of, 121–22; notes to, 15; optimism in, 16; and Rousseau, 34

Bataille, Henry, 67

Beckett, Samuel: and eros, 56, 64; and religion, 157 n.28

Bernardini Napoletano, Francesca: on *Cosmicomiche*, 19, 66; on demystification, 24; on engagement, 24, 29; on satire, 24; on *Ti con Zero*, 19

Borges, Jorge Luis, 45–46, 130, 163 n.24

Boselli, Mario: letter to Calvino, 122

171